D0355860

A Tale of Two Melons

Emperor and Subject in Ming China

A Tale of Two Melons

Emperor and Subject in Ming China

Sarah Schneewind

Hackett Publishing Company, Inc.
Indianapolis/Cambridge

Copyright © 2006 by Hackett Publishing Company, Inc.

All rights reserved
Printed in the United States of America

11 10 09 08 07 06   1 2 3 4 5 6

For further information, please address:

Hackett Publishing Company, Inc.
P.O. Box 44937
Indianapolis, IN 46244-0937

www.hackettpublishing.com

Cover design by Abigail Coyle
Text design by Carrie Wagner
Printed at Edwards Brothers, Inc.

Library of Congress Cataloging-in-Publication Data

Schneewind, Sarah.
A tale of two melons: emperor and subject in Ming China / Sarah
Schneewind.
     p. cm.
Includes bibliographical references.
ISBN-13: 978-0-87220-825-4 (hbk.)
ISBN-13: 978-0-87220-824-7 (pbk.)
ISBN-10: 0-87220-825-7 (hbk.)
ISBN-10: 0-87220-824-9 (pbk.)
1. China–Social conditions–960-1644. 2. China—History—Ming dynasty,
1368–1644. I. Title. II. Title: Emperor and subject in Ming China.
HN733.S35 2006
306.0951'09023–dc22

                                                                2006016375

The paper in this publication meets the minimum requirements of
American National Standard for Information Sciences—
Permanence of Paper for Printed Library Materials,
ANSI Z39.48-1984

∞

For Bruce

Contents

Acknowledgments

In the course of this project I was fortunate enough to experience the magic of connecting old texts with real places and live people. Dallas-based businessman Felix Chen gave me a grant to go to Nanjing and Jurong in the spring of 2004. Jurong people, from the mayor, to journalists, to restaurant owners, were most welcoming. I visited local sites and talked with men of the Yitai Zhang (who were baffled yet pleased to see a foreign woman studying their ancestors). My hosts were Zhai Zhonghua, the head of the Jurong Museum, and Wen Dezhong of the municipal government's cultural bureau. Mr. Zhai gave generously of his time and his knowledge, searching through the county archives for me and lending me a beautiful office in the reconstructed Qing academy that houses the museum's steles, archaeological exhibits, and display of traditional agricultural tools. Both Mr. Wen's standard Chinese (the local accent takes a little getting used to) and his willingness to start conversations with total strangers possibly surnamed Zhang were invaluable.

As well as these new friends, I would like to thank Pei-yi Wu, who helped me struggle through the first translation of the emperor's preface and ode about thirteen years ago. Xiaofei Kang helped with some of the translations in this book more recently. I am grateful to Zvi Ben Dor Benite, Laurie Dennis (who is writing a novel about Ming Taizu), Alexis McCrossen, J. B. Schneewind, Martha Schulman, Bruce Tindall, and the late Jaret Weisfogel for their careful comments. I also thank colleagues at the Southwest Conference on Asian Studies (San Marcos, 2000), the Association for Asian Studies (San Diego, 2004), and the International Association of the Historians of Asia (Taipei, 2004), especially Peter Ditmanson, and my editor, Deborah Wilkes. Remaining errors are, of course, my responsibility.

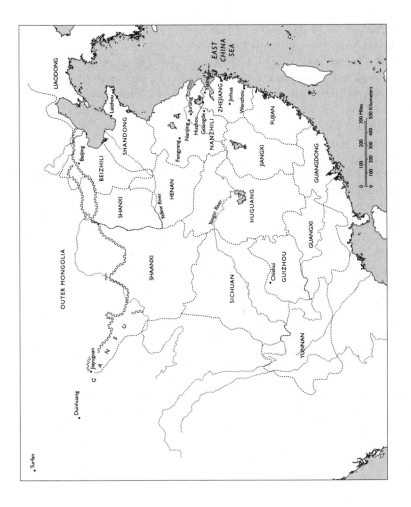

Map of Ming China

Introduction

Writing history is like making a collage picture. With a question about the past in mind, the historian searches through the various documents that survive from a place and time—China during the Ming period (1368–1644), for instance. Some of the texts will discuss aspects of life in the past that address the historian's question. Most of what he or she finds will not bear directly on it, and will be set aside. And some texts will offer up pieces of the past that lead to other questions. (This book grew out of my idle curiosity at a title I ran across while looking for texts by the founder of the Ming dynasty about the villages of China.) As the historian finds facts, he fits them together to form a picture of what life was like at a certain time in the past. The picture includes narrative, in which people and events move forward through time. It includes explanation of the causes and effects of those events. And it includes analysis, in which events that occurred at different times or places are grouped together and explained. At every step, the historian is looking, choosing, discarding, and arranging to understand more than any single text can tell him. The texts must be accessible to others, so that they can check his facts, and the picture he creates must fit with other facts and patterns, so that we can be sure that they truly illuminate some aspect of the past.

The historian also has to keep in mind that the texts he works with are not simply fragments of the past. Every text was written for a purpose and presents events and people in a certain way. The keeping of records in China began with noting the results of divinations on matters regarding the Shang (c. 1600–1045 B.C.) royal family, military affairs, and the weather and harvest. In the Zhou period (1045–256 B.C.), the proclamations of the Zhou kings were recorded, and histories of earlier monarchs were fabricated, in what became the classic *Book of History* or *Book of Documents*. The speeches of ministers, along with political and military events, were also recorded in the *Zuo zhuan*. The Qin dynasty (221–207 B.C.), as it created a unified bureaucratic empire, asserted control over writing as well as standardizing laws and punishments, weights and measures. Writing history was a way for the government to control what events meant, even when it could not control the events themselves. As historiographical (history-writing) traditions took shape in the Han period (207 B.C.–220 A.D.) and after, histories produced by scholars working in the imperial government included basic annals of key events, biographies, and essays on particular topics. In the Tang period (618–907), official historians were instructed not to

> give false praise, or conceal evil, but [instead] write a straight account of events. The portents of heaven, earth, sun and moon, the distribution of mountains and rivers, fiefs and cities, the precedence between junior and senior lines of descent, ritual and military affairs, changes of reward and punishment, between prosperity and decline, all should be first recorded. The historians should base themselves on the Court Diary and the Record of Administrative Affairs, setting this out in chronological form and incorporating the principles of praise and blame.[1]

History was to be based on records that were kept on a daily basis, and on reports from other offices.

The Ministry of Rites reported fortunate omens every quarter. The astronomer royal, who constructed the calendar, also kept track of heavenly portents. Tribute-bearing missions from foreign countries were recorded. Records were kept of changes in the music used at sacrifices. The Ministry of Finance reported changes to administrative divisions of territory; the outcome of harvests, whether good or bad; the effects of natural disasters and subsequent relief efforts; and "the granting of marks of distinction to 'filial and righteous families.'" The Ministry of Justice recorded legal changes. Unusual evidence of good local administration, and exemplary people such as "eminent scholars, men of unusual ability, great men, retired scholars, righteous husbands, and chaste widows," were all to be reported. These records were all used by the historians, but they were never raw facts. Everyone understood that moral judgment, political power, and the smooth functioning of the cosmos were at stake in these various aspects of governance, so reports at all levels, right up to the dynastic histories, had built-in didactic functions.[2] Often described as a mirror reflecting current events, history created meaning and power, and historiographical practices favored the survival of certain types of sources and facts: what we have to work with today. Except for the Shang oracle bones, which were dug up and deciphered only in the twentieth century, these records of the Chinese past were also part of the mental furniture of Ming writers.

Even apart from historians, each person who wrote any kind of text was already looking around him, selecting and discarding, and creating meaning out of events large and small, contemporary views, and his own mind. And for every person who wrote down something about his own times—whether it was a eulogy to be buried with a beloved mother, or a commercial manual of advice for gardeners, or an account of the great southward crossing of the Yangzi River that led the founder of the Ming dynasty to victory over his rivals—there were thousands who never wrote a word. Yet those people too created meaning in their own lives. Whether in a mundane way by chatting about the day at supper with the family, or by making ambitious or heroic choices that led them far from home, or by explaining suffering they could not escape, even people who have left no written traces contributed to the shape of the past by creating stories about themselves within the framework of contemporary beliefs and institutions. The raw materials of the historian are like the raw materials of the collage artist. The historian cuts texts up and rearranges them, trying to make a true picture of a time and place, but they were first created by someone else for a different purpose.

In the middle of the fourteenth century, the Black Death swept through Eurasia. Families were decimated, and people turned to religion for answers. Millenarian movements and rebel warlords arose to challenge the Mongol Yuan dynasty, which had ruled North China since 1234 and the South too since 1279. The final victor in the prolonged and complicated civil war was a self-made man, Zhu Yuanzhang 朱元璋 (the surname comes first in Chinese). Born in 1328 to a poor farmer in the impoverished Huai region north of the Yangzi River, Zhu had lost nearly all his family members to plague in 1344, had begged for his rice as a wandering Buddhist novice for a while, and had then joined the millenarian Red Turban rebels. He proved to be a military genius, and a charismatic leader who attracted smart advisors. In 1368 he defeated rival warlords and the remnants of the Yuan dynasty, and declared himself the first emperor of a new dynasty, the Ming (Bright).

Zhu Yuanzhang named his reign era the Hongwu, or "Abundantly Martial," so he is sometimes called "the Hongwu emperor," but usually he is referred to by his posthumous title, Ming Taizu (Great Ancestor of the Ming, also written "T'ai-tsu"). His power and authority began with military strength, but to consolidate it he created both an institutional framework for governing the country and an ideological framework in which people understood themselves as his subjects. Moreover, his vision for China went far beyond military control: more of a social engineer than any other Chinese ruler before Mao Zedong, Zhu planned a stable, peaceful, agrarian society free of the poverty, class conflict, and chaos in which he had grown up. Taizu's ideal society was composed of small farms in harmonious villages, where obedient men and women worked to feed and clothe their parents and children and pay their taxes, neither producing for the market nor leaving home to work elsewhere.[3]

Following long precedent Ming Taizu created an official bureaucracy headquartered in the capital, Nanjing, and with an office in every county. The bureaucracy put the resources of the empire at Taizu's disposal. Educated men were gathered in and ranked, and then sent out again with specific mandates to administer the approximately 80 million subjects and 1.5 million square miles of the empire. Taxes paid in grain, money, and cloth poured into the capital. Texts poured in too: official reports on all the kinds of subjects mentioned above and more, evaluations of officials by their supervisors, impeachments of corrupt officials, memorials by educated men suggesting policies or just flattering the emperor in hopes of winning an official position, petitions from communities in need of famine relief, and so on. Counties specializing in particular products sent them in as tribute to the throne. Bricks for the new Nanjing city wall, and labor to build it with, were gathered in. Outside the capital, people were moved to uncultivated land, counted and registered, assigned to places and professions, and organized into groups for policing, worship, taxation, and labor duties. The deities of the empire, too, were reported and categorized, their sacrifices were regularized, and a calendar of ceremonies at each level of administration was fixed.

The government bureaucracy managed all these people, products, and texts with reams of paper files, assigning each to its proper place. The ability to categorize, to order, to collect, and to display, physically and in texts, the products and peoples of the empire both showed and strengthened the court's preeminence and the sacred centrality of the capital. Robert Campany calls this understanding of the world as centered on the capital a "locative" mode of cosmography.[4] The Ming state, and the dynastic founder in particular, were tremendously powerful, with the bureaucracy and its ideological machinery at the emperor's command. People at all social levels were affected by the state and understood themselves partially in terms of it. Yet it is equally evident that as texts and products passed from the localities to the court and back, it took action on both sides to make the exchanges happen. Men had to present themselves to take the exams; accurate reports were essential in managing resources and people; cloth and bricks could only be acquired through local cooperation. Even the basic tasks of government that kept the dynasty in power—tax collection and prevention of rebellion—entailed compromises with society. Although they are harder for the historian to see, the locals and intermediaries essential to the exchanges of empire were acting on sophisticated motives and understandings of their own.

The ruler was central, but he was hardly all-powerful. Much of the history written about the Ming period has focused on the center. The story of the early Ming period has been a story of how Taizu set the stage for subsequent developments by reshaping the central government to concentrate power in his own hands; established new social institutions in every village of his vast empire; closed China's borders to foreign trade and hence to innovative influences; and promoted an insular, agrarian, Han-nativist popular morality. Taizu has been called not only despotic, but even totalitarian. His power to impose his will on Chinese state and society has been an axiom of history, frequently used to explain later phenomena. The fall of the Ming dynasty 246 years after Taizu's death, for instance, has been blamed on his abolition of the post of grand councilor (prime minister), which left the scholar-officials without a legitimate chief spokesman. Certainly, up on the great Zhonghua gate of the Nanjing city wall, a vast brick and stone structure whose interior tunnels could harbor 3,000 soldiers, Taizu's power is still palpable. The difficult task for the historian is to assess the extent and nature of Taizu's power fairly, realizing that he may have had great power in some arenas and little in others.

By 1500 at the latest, Taizu's vision for society had failed. True, most of China's people still worked as farmers, but increasingly they specialized in crops grown for market. Rooted in the amazingly productive agriculture of the South, where three or four crops a year might be grown on the same land and where cheap water transport made trade easy, the commercial economy boomed, sharpening class divisions. The China of the late sixteenth century, particularly its cities, would have appalled the Ming founder. Every kind of good and service was bought and sold, including people of all ages and sexes. Plays and operas drew crowds of onlookers; even upper-class women secluded in their homes read poetry and pornographic novels alongside Buddhist scriptures and Confucian lessons. Celebrity courtesans, more like today's movie stars than like prostitutes (of whom there were also plenty) entertained upper-class men, mingled with respectable married women, and set fashion trends that the city-dwellers eagerly followed. Educated families spent fortunes on collections: teapots, for instance, or decorated inksticks. Their fortunes were made in office, in usury, and in production and commerce, domestic and international. Across the continent in Jacobean England, playwright Ben Jonson had a salesboy ask, "What is't you buy? Veary fine China stuffes [fabrics] of all kindes and quallityes? China chaynes, China bracelets, China scarfes, China fannes, China girdles, China knives, China boxes, China cabinets."[5] The powerful Earl of Northampton slept in an elaborately decorated Chinese lacquer bed, of the kind Taizu had once destroyed to show his hatred for luxurious display. Not only royalty, but the subjects of Ming China, like those of contemporary Tudor and Stuart England, collected and displayed the products of the whole Ming empire in their homes.[6]

But we need not look as far ahead as the late Ming period to see that Taizu's power to shape and control society was limited. His own writings cast a different light even on the early Ming period. Although he launched vigorous campaigns against bribery and graft, officials and their clerks frequently engaged in the kind of petty corruption considered by one historian to be "the bitter melon" of the traditional system, able to spread and reroot even under Taizu's stern rule.[7] The emperor found both state and society recalcitrant. He repeatedly set up systems of village governance that did not work; he repeatedly found that the personnel implementing orders resisted him and had to be replaced. Halfway through his reign, Taizu wrote: "Despite my exhaustive efforts, I'm unable to transform bad people, whether they are smart or stupid. What I mean is, I set up some law to get rid of villainy and corruption, always for the sake of preserving the subject people. . . . Yet even after a long time, nothing produces any results. Alas, how hard it is!"[8]

Not only did Taizu ultimately fail to tame the Chinese economy, the engine that drove the early modern world, not only did he in his own time face great disobedience; he could not even unilaterally control the institutional or ideological framework of rule. When Zhu Yuanzhang took the throne, he claimed to have received the "Mandate of Heaven (*tian ming* 天命)": a divine seal of approval based on his virtue. Unlike Japanese emperors, the rulers of China could not claim an unbroken line of descent from a supreme deity; in fact, the posthumous title by which he is usually known, Ming Taizu, signals precisely that Zhu was founding a brand-new dynasty, and it was well known that he was the son of poor farmers. Chinese political theory held that the ruler—whether he had gained power through war, through a coup d'état, or through recognized succession—had been chosen by Heaven. Heaven was sometimes understood as an impersonal cosmic principle, sometimes as more interventionist high deity. (The same word, *tian*, also just means "sky.") One of the emperor's duties was to sacrifice to Heaven. So long as the ruler carried out the proper ceremonies, safeguarded the people's livelihood, consulted with wise and good advisers, practiced personal virtue, and recognized virtue in others, Heaven would see that the cosmos ran smoothly, and the ruling dynasty would be legitimate. But if the ruler failed, Heaven's Mandate could pass to a new hero founding a new dynasty. Unlike the European doctrine of the "divine right of kings," the Mandate checked, as well as validated, the monarch's exercise of power.

Taizu fitted himself into the cognitive model of the Mandate of Heaven. He was a deeply religious man, and took his role very seriously indeed. Late in life, he wrote family instructions to his descendants, hoping against hope that they would take their role seriously too.

> When a ruler first gains the realm it is because Heaven has chosen a man of virtue. As for [his successors], if they are constantly reverential toward Heaven and take to heart their ancestor's concern for the realm, they can receive Heaven's blessing forever. If they begin to be negligent disaster will result. . . . Only when concern is always on your mind will the people be at peace and the state secure. What you shall be concerned about is that the winds and rain come in the proper season and the

> fields have a bumper harvest so that the people will be
> assured of their livelihood.[9]

Taizu went on to recommend tax remissions for disaster areas, and for poor areas when possible. He stressed testing officials by giving them duties and dismissing or rewarding them according to their performance. He enjoined absolute sincerity in carrying out the sacrificial rituals to the various deities, care in following rules of etiquette, and prudence in listening to reports from all quarters. And he urged personal virtues of which Ben Franklin would have approved:

> Little wine shall be drunk. Meals shall be taken on time
> and not too much shall be eaten after noon. . . . Do not
> associate too freely with actors and actresses. Do not sing
> drunkenly or carry on drinking at night. . . . When the
> evening court is over, retire. Get up when the morning
> star is out. When you are not sick, never be lazy. This is
> the way to show respect for Heaven and Man and it is
> the way to make the nation prosperous.[10]

The ideology of the Mandate of Heaven did not succeed in holding Ming rulers to these high standards of personal or governmental virtue, any more than Taizu's contemporaries in England, Edward III and Richard II, lived up to the teachings of Jesus Christ. But insofar as the ideology of the Mandate demanded the acquiescence of the common people and the cooperation of educated men, it meant that the Ming dynasty depended on its officials and subjects imagining themselves part of the enterprise of the new regime at the helm of an old state. While he set precedents in some ways, Taizu was working within traditions, social relations, and webs of meaning from which he was never completely able to cut free.

But this was not a democratic system; it was not that the people had the right to decide whether the emperor was doing a good job. Rather, if all was well, Heaven would signal that fact. The prime theoretician of imperial Confucian rule, Dong Zhongshu (c. 175– c. 105 B.C.), wrote in the Han period, "When the sovereign is such that the people unanimously turn to him as to their father and mother, the auspicious omens of Heaven appear as a response to his sincerity."[11] If he ruled poorly, unlucky signs would appear, such as monstrous births and comets. A few missteps would not destroy the ruler's moral authority. But a pattern of corruption or ineptitude, either of the ruler himself or among his officials, could. Every serious rebellion or natural disaster carried with it the possibility that the ruler was in the wrong, that Heaven had turned against him, and that political power was about to change hands. Of course, the ruler could try to pass the buck. In 1455, Taizu's great-great-grandson the Jingtai emperor announced to the sacred Mount Tai:

> If it is by my faults that I have drawn down calamities, assuredly I do not decline the personal responsibility, but for the turning of misfortune to good fortune it is truly you, oh god, who has the duty to apply yourself to it. If a fault has been committed and you do not perform a commendable act, you will be as guilty as I. If, on the other hand, you transform misfortune into good fortune, who will be able to equal your merit?[12]

Heaven, Earth, and Man—all three understood as both physical and spiritual entities—were interdependent. Human happenings could be caused by, reflected in, or foretold by heavenly or earthly happenings. Some people understood the linkage as conscious: that the deities Heaven and Earth purposely sent messages to humans by producing oddities. Other people thought that the anomalies, just like the normal products and processes of the cosmos, resulted from natural resonances between humanity and the natural world. The two equal and opposite forces of the universe, yang and yin *qi* 氣 (energy or substance), combined to produce normal plants, animals, and humans as well as strange phenomena. Anomalies were, in Erik Zürcher's words, "amazing, exceptional, and charged with deep significance, but . . . very much part of the natural order of things."[13]

Portents like comets or earthquakes, or the birth of deformed animals, nearly everyone agreed, were warning signals: signs that someone was suffering great injustice, that government was not protecting the common people, that the ruler was not listening to advice, or even that the ruler was downright wicked. A famous example of heavenly response occurs in a play about a young widow unjustly accused of murdering a ruffian who tried to force his son and himself on her and her mother-in-law. The widow makes a false confession to spare her mother-in-law the ordeal of judicial torture. Heaven signals the miscarriage of justice with a fall of snow on the hot summer day when she is beheaded and punishes the whole county with a three-year drought.[14] But there was no code book for interpreting portents: in other cases a fall of snow in summer meant that rebels were plotting. Even when everyone agreed that a portent was a warning or a chastisement, it was not clear who had stimulated it.[15] On the other hand, good weather and abundant harvests, and propitious anomalies—like the appearance of a unicorn (*qilin* 麒麟), a fall of sweet dew, or rice stems with two heads of grain—signaled prosperity under virtuous government. Heaven, Earth, and Man were closely connected, and often it was the ruler who connected them. Anomalies were meaningful messages that signaled the rightful retention or impending transfer of the Mandate of Heaven.

But the imperial state was not the only framework within which meaning was constructed; it was not the only carrier of moral authority. Confucianism, Buddhism, and Daoism (also spelled Taoism) were all traditions that could contribute to state ideology, but that also explained life outside the framework of the state. Confucianism focused as much on the family as on the state as a fundamental, cosmically important institution of human life. Confucian virtues tied together the different parts of society. In 1211, for instance, one Wu Ruming was honored by the government. It was recorded that

> Ruming's [family] have lived for many generations without dividing. They are compassionate, filial and friendly. When his mother was ill he cut his thigh [to make her medicine] and she was completely cured. Auspicious mushrooms have appeared at the side of the house where he lives. When locusts devastated the area, they did not devour his family's harvest; and he used it to relieve the famine, so saving many lives. Strange trees grow together at his gateway. People call them "trees of righteousness."[16]

Buddhism validated the individual's search for salvation, whether as a layperson or within a monastery or nunnery, and the religion rewarded good deeds done for family and community. Buddhist doctrine holds that all existence is illusory. The original Indian teaching demanded that the serious spiritual seeker leave the family and devote his or her life to meditation, so that he or she could recognize the illusory nature of the world. That understanding would free the seeker from the wheel of perpetual rebirth into the world, with its inevitable suffering. But most Chinese people saw enlightenment and the liberating dissolution of the self called "nirvana" as a very far-off goal. Most focused instead on improving their karma, so as to improve their lot in the next life. As an abbot explained to a prostitute in a late Ming story:

> What went before is the cause and what follows is the effect. The doing is the cause, the results are the effect. In the saying, "Plant melons and you get melons; sow beans and you get beans," the planting and sowing is the cause and what you get is the effect... If you want to know the cause in your previous life, look at the effect in this life. If you want to know the effect in your next life, look at what you've done in this life.[17]

Just as the emperor had recorders standing to his left and right to take down his words for posterity in the Court Diary, each person had two little boys recording his or her every good and evil deed to report to the king of the underworld, or so one Buddhist scripture explained.[18] A person's actions and intentions affected his fate, or "ming," the same term as used for Heaven's "Mandate." Ming people understood their lives partly in terms of a balance book of good and bad deeds.[19] Exchange worked in the popular religion too. Deities would answer prayers for health, wealth, and children, and worshippers would repay them with sacrifices and honor.

Finally, Daoists pursued spiritual calm and emotional distance from worldly matters, longevity, magic powers of flight into realms of transcendent beauty, alchemy, and secret knowledge. Daoists—"men of the Way"—were marvelous figures in the Ming imagination. One story tells of immortals who descended to earth in disguise and opened relations with a human family.

> The visitors sat down and watched the old man go to the back of the garden, where, with his fingers, he dug out a sweet melon from under the snow. It was indeed a melon
>
> > With green leaves, a tender stalk,
> > And yellow flowers blooming at the top.
> > From its pungent source rose its fragrance;
> > From bitterness came its sweet taste.

> ...The old man took a knife and peeled the melon
> and cut off the top, letting out an extraordinary fra-
> grance... "How very strange!" they exclaimed. How
> could he have grown such sweet melons in such heavy
> snow?[20]

Only at the end of the story does the family understand the old gar-
dener's powers, symbolized by his control over his own little domain,
the garden. A Portuguese friar who visited China in the middle of
the sixteenth century reported:

> There are in the kingdom of Taybin [that is, Da Ming
> (Great Ming)] two kinds of friars after their manner of
> religion, some who do not eat meat nor eggs nor fish, but
> sustain themselves only with rice, herbs and fruits. Many
> of these live like hermits, like one we saw on a hill adjoin-
> ing the wall of Hocchiu [Fuzhou city]. He was in a tiny
> little grot with three little idols therein, and he looked as
> if he was wrapped in contemplation. Around his cell was
> his little garden which he had planted with gourds,
> cucumbers, water-melons, egg-plants and other vegeta-
> bles, and there was a brook of running water. On the
> outside, it was bounded by a high and thick cane planta-
> tion [probably bamboo], being distant about an arque-
> bus-shot from the houses of the town.[21]

Living outside family and town, such hermits and mystics considered
themselves independent of authority. Daoist hagiographer Ge Hong
葛洪 (283–343) wrote that one Daoist adept declared his way supe-
rior to the way of kings, and unattainable by them. And another
vanished instantly when a Han emperor told him: "You are my
subject."[22] Such Daoists, like earnest Confucians and enlightened
Buddhists, had their own legitimacy in people's eyes: that is why
Ming Taizu invented fabulous tales about Daoist masters who
assisted him as part of building up his own authority.[23] Flame-throw-
ers and cannon had helped him to *take* power, but in order to *keep*
it, he needed legitimacy.

The possibility for moral authority outside of the framework of the
state meant that in creating meaning out of the seeming jumble of
reality, people saw messages for themselves, not just for the ruler, in
strange plants, animals, birds, and so on. People could interpret

anomalies within any or all of China's religious frameworks.[24] For Confucians, nature and cosmos might resonate with good or bad governance at the center, but also with a good county official, a powerful local family, or a son who devotedly carried out his filial duty to his parents, like the Wu Ruming described above. In a Buddhist framework, omens signaled the state of a person's karma, the presence of a saving saint, or even the arrival of a messiah. In the 1330s, in Zhu Yuanzhang's disaster-stricken native area, for instance, many people had looked for the coming of the Buddha of the future to usher in a new utopia. To Daoists, anomalies could reveal the secrets of the universe, with no reference to politics. And the nonsectarian popular religion could understand odd happenings and grand symbols as referring to someone as humble as a farm bride. The *qilin* or unicorn, for instance, whose rare appearance was a sign of imperial virtue, was also thought to answer prayers for sons. It appeared as a motif on items made for dowries up through the twentieth century.[25] The statue of a *qilin* at the tomb of Ming Taizu's parents has its right front leg worn away where women have scraped at the stone to make a potion that would assure them male offspring.

Lives could be lived and meanings could be created independent of the central state. And to interact effectively with localities and retain the Mandate of Heaven, the center had to take those local frameworks into account. The Ming empire was not just shaped from the top down, but was woven together by exchanges between locality and capital, by the efforts and contributions of millions of people. The stuff of these exchanges included grain and other material goods, the labor of back and brain, the signs and symbols of honor, and texts expressing understandings of the world and one's place in it.

So. One fine day in 1372, a strange gift arrived at the imperial palace . . .

Chapter I

On a Lacquer Tray

It was the middle of an ordinary day: July 28, 1372. Ming Taizu, in his palace in the capital, Nanjing, was interrupted just as he was hoping to get some work done. His ceremonial dawn meeting with the officials who staffed the imperial court and the central government had ended. Now Taizu wanted to turn to his paperwork: the stacks of reports and suggestions from officials all over the country that embodied the work of government.[1] To his surprise and annoyance, a group of high officials, led by Minister of Rites Tao Kai 陶凱, entered the room. They wore such solemn expressions that Taizu thought they had come to admonish him for some failing, some action contrary to virtuous government—again! Instead, they presented him with a pair of ripe melons. They were not cut and covered with a napkin, as melons were supposed to be when served to the emperor; they just sat there baldly on a lacquer tray, with their joined stems sticking up.[2]

No wonder the emperor was surprised! Taizu tells us:

> At first I only knew there were melons and did not understand what was up. The minister [Tao Kai] reported: "The melons grew from the same stalk!" When I heard this, I thought it was really strange. I tried asking how this was understood in former dynasties. The group of ministers one after another said, "Several emperors of former dynasties had them, and called them lucky omens. Now, when Your Majesty is ruling, melons growing from the same stalk have been produced in Jurong. Well, Jurong is the emperor's ancestral home. It goes without saying that this is a good omen!" The group of ministers made pretty speeches like this.[3]

In making their "pretty speeches," the officials were drawing on the long tradition in which odd plants and animals, and celestial, terrestrial, and weather phenomena could all be understood as having meaning for human affairs. Although the ministers said that the meaning of the pair of melons was self-evident, when we read Taizu's own account of the audience in which they were presented, and compare it to two other eye-witness accounts, it becomes clear that there was disagreement over how to interpret the melons. The story was retold over several hundred years by authors who had further interpretations. My research into the place where the melons were grown and the family of the man who grew them suggests yet another interpretation, one that sheds light on the nature of the Ming regime. This chapter will introduce the three primary accounts—one by Taizu, one in a court history, and one by a top adviser—and explain why the ministers interrupted the emperor's morning paperwork with a tray of fruit.

Taizu recounted the presentation of the melons in a preface to an ode that describes and praises them. His preface focuses on his own words and thoughts, which the next chapter will explore, and records the ministers' side of the conversation only briefly. In Taizu's version, for instance, Tao Kai says only four words—*gua sheng tong di* 瓜生同蒂—in the frugal language of classical Chinese: "The melons grew from the same stalk!" The emperor did not deign to record the names or titles of the other officials present, although they had been his close colleagues in the slow conquest of the empire. The two other accounts were written by officials who reported the ministers' side of the conversation more fully and the emperor's side differently. The *Veritable Records of the Reign of Ming Taizu* drew on an immediate eye-witness account of the audience, but took its final shape some thirty years later as part of the routine historiographical work of the dynasty. Based on court diaries and reports from the empire, the *Veritable Records* of each reign were compiled by scholars under the next reigning emperor. The records of the first Ming reign are notoriously unreliable. They were designed by the scholar Xie Jin to legitimate Taizu's fourth son, the Yongle emperor Zhu Di, who usurped his nephew's throne in 1402 to make himself the third Ming ruler.[4] Like Taizu's own essay and the third account of the melon audience discussed on page 5, the account in the *Veritable Records* omitted parts of the conversation and may have falsified other parts. Nonetheless, such imperfect records are all historians usually have. Different accounts, when read against each other, give a more complete view of what actually happened in the audience. But we can also look at differences in the accounts to think about what each author was using the melon incident for. History includes not only the study of the facts of the past, but also the study of why the sources recording those facts were written and preserved.

So, why did the ministers—busy men trying to get a vast new empire up and running—think the melons were important? According to the *Veritable Records*, Tao Kai, as head of the bureau in charge of ritual, religion, and the civil service examinations, explained to Taizu: "Melons from one stalk were produced at Jurong. Jurong is Your Majesty's ancestral home. It really is a good omen. Now because sagely virtue has united the whole country in harmony, the auspicious omen of two melons sharing a stalk is manifesting Your Majesty's benevolence in protecting the people and cherishing the ten thousand creatures. It is not accidental!"[5] Tao interprets the double melons as arising from the harmony of the whole country under the benevolent reign of Zhu Yuanzhang. Peace and national unity were indeed considerable—and recent—accomplishments.

Unity began with military control. Only four or five years earlier, Ming Taizu and his generals had emerged victorious from the long civil war. The Ming empire was also politically unified; unlike contemporary Europe where local power was largely hereditary, and not closely controlled by the monarchies, the whole Ming empire was governed from the capital through bureaucrats appointed for short terms to places far from their homes. Under the leadership of the emperor, six functional ministries (Rites, Revenue, Personnel, Public Works, War, and Justice) and smaller agencies in charge of such matters as judicial review, astronomy, medicine, and horses were coordinated until 1380 by a Secretariat headed by grand councilors. A watch-dog agency called the Censorate reported on officials throughout the bureaucracy and even remonstrated with the emperor himself. There was also a think tank of the brightest scholars, called the Hanlin Academy.[6] Officials were sent to carry out imperial policy in every one of some 1,500 subprefectures and counties, and local men were selected and authorized to link the villages with the counties. As peace returned and the infrastructure was rebuilt, the economy recovered; as discussed in the Introduction, a united national market would eventually emerge to become a driving force in the world. At the midpoint of the Ming period, 120 years after the melon audience, Columbus set out to seek Chinese goods (and, incidentally, brought the New World its first melon seeds), and in the late

Ming dynasty the Spanish poured Mexican silver into China to buy them. So unity was military, political, and economic, and now that the whole Chinese-culture area was under ethnic Chinese rule for the first time since 1127, Taizu was also determined to create a unified society by eliminating Mongolian customs, assigning each family to a hereditary occupation, imposing community rituals, and promoting moral codes that drew on Confucianism, Buddhism, and popular beliefs in ghosts and spirits.[7] His dynasty lasted; his social design did not.

Unification was founded on military conquest. But, as Tao Kai's words remind us, Taizu could hold the throne only through popular and divine acquiescence: the Mandate of Heaven. The ministers certainly felt justified in interrupting his morning's work to present such a good sign that Taizu in fact held the Mandate. Recording omens had long been part of the basic work of officialdom. Dynastic histories began with basic annals of key events that included omens and portents, understood as, in one historian's words, "supernatural 'comment' on the exercise of authority."[8] It was, in fact, critical to a dynasty's survival that such signs be correctly understood. Moreover, earlier emperors had usually been delighted to receive and publicize such omens as double-headed grain, tortoises with writing on their shells, and rainbow-colored clouds. But—*melons*? Taizu was skeptical, and he asked how earlier dynasties had understood double melons.

The emperor's request for instruction was quite proper. Although the officials said that the omen was easy to understand, interpreting anomalies was in fact a tricky business. Heaven was a deity or force very different from the interventionist God who gave Moses and Muhammad their explicit instructions. Heaven did not speak. The sages of old had uncovered its patterns, governed in accord with them, and tried to record them in the classics: the *Book of Songs* (also called the *Book of Odes*); the historical work the *Spring and Autumn Annals*; the *Book of Documents* (also called *Book of History*); the *Record of Rites* (*Liji*), which described rituals appropriate to each season and situation; and the *Book of Changes* (*Yijing*), used to divine propitious times for action. But the classics left plenty of room for disagreement on how to understand the moral order established by Heaven.

Moreover, discerning Heaven's will in any particular case was difficult, and one sign of an emperor's virtue was his willingness to accept explanations and guidance from the scholar-officials attending him. They had won their places in government because of their deep and wide knowledge of history, literature, and the classics of Confucian thought, knowledge that had shaped them into virtuous and thoughtful persons. As bureaucrats, officials enforced imperial law, but as scholars they guided the emperor in carrying out Heaven's will. Occasionally, this meant drawing on their classical knowledge and the present circumstances to interpret anomalies as omens. Tao Kai's interpretation is straightforward and typical of such occasions: he reminds the emperor of the Mandate of Heaven and flatters him by saying that he has truly attained it. Two further interpretations of the double melons offered by officials at the time are more complicated, as we shall see.

The third contemporary version of the melon incident is an eye-witness account of the audience by one of Taizu's long-time top advisers, Song Lian 宋濂 (1310–1381). Song Lian was one of a group of Confucian thinkers who had seen in Zhu Yuanzhang the potential for being the absolute ruler they thought would end the violence and social disorder of the late Yuan period. Song argued that effective government would obviate all rebellion and crime by being so complete as to seem natural, and that the ruler's mind should in fact be aligned with natural patterns. In Song's view, as paraphrased by John W. Dardess:

> When the ruler instructs his people, his efforts should radiate with the luminosity of the sun and moon. When he is pleased, he must communicate his pleasure in such a way that the people are made to think of auspicious clouds and felicitous breezes. His anger should have the sudden and startling effect of thunder and lightning. When he acts to foster life and productivity, these acts must penetrate and nourish as sweet rain and dew; and when he deals in death, the effect should be as devastating as that of an ice storm or frost on vegetation.[9]

From about 1358, when Taizu passed through Jinhua, a center of Confucian studies at the time, Song Lian served him as an adviser and writer.

Song Lian's account of the melon audience stars not Tao Kai but a different minister, Grand Councilor Wang Guangyang 汪廣洋 (d. 1380), an upright and serious scholar who had worked with Taizu since 1355. Wang took advantage of Taizu's question about the history of auspicious melons to flaunt his erudition. He quoted almost word-for-word a passage from a history of the Han dynasty that notes numerous vegetable omens: two or more ears of grain growing from one stalk, several stalks producing one head of grain, trees that grow together, and eight cases of auspicious melons (*jia gua* 嘉瓜).[10] Wang then referred briefly to a memorial by Tang statesman and literary master Han Yu (768–824), a report explaining to the Tang emperor the connection of the ruler with vegetable omens. Han Yu had written:

> When the kingly one's virtue reaches the earth, then auspicious grain is produced. Prostrate, I consider that Your Majesty's way harmonizes Heaven and Earth, and grace drenches animals and plants. Nothing nearby fails to cooperate; nothing distant fails to honor. Spirits and humans are in accord; wind and rain come in season. The aforementioned auspicious grain and other such phenomena, like two roots joining to make one plant, or two ovaries producing one flower [or one ovary producing two flowers] or like extended tendrils blossoming, or different fruits on the same stem, all convey congratulations on harmony and also express the blessing of an abundant harvest.[11]

By referring to Han Yu's report, Wang Guangyang asserted that auspicious melons were a standard omen and offered the new ruler a connection with the glorious Tang dynasty. Wang continued: "There have always been such lucky omens in response [to good governance]. Your Majesty's energetic spirit of rule has exceeded that of the Han dynasty and surpassed that of the Tang dynasty. Therefore, Heaven has bestowed this precious tally, in which we see the image and reality of the Great Peace."[12] Historical precedent, as Wang presented it, not only validated the authenticity of the omen, but served as a prelude to the Ming founder's own achievements.

Song Lian further reports that the other ministers joined in Wang's praise of the emperor. They also referred to earlier heavenly responses to Taizu himself. Song Lian's hymn of praise, which follows his prose account of the conversation, reports:

> The group of ministers all said,
> Bowing and kowtowing,

"Divine peace is thus/sproutingly manifested:
Long live the Son of Heaven!
Now, following the founding of the dynasty,
the numinous bestowals have come one after another:
double-headed grain,
joint-calyx pregnant lotus,
and now in addition this divine tally.
Recently, under the emperor's rule
Kingly transformation [has occurred] of itself nearby
while distant regions all submit."[13]

Like Han Yu's memorial and Wang's speech, this hymn offers blatant flattery, often part of the relationship between minister and ruler. But these statements were also propaganda in the making, drafts of public relations bulletins that the ruler could use to strengthen his government's legitimacy.[14] Song Lian explains that rulers from the antique paragon the Duke of Zhou onward had all commemorated and publicized their omens. Song requests that Taizu order the history officials to prepare a true account (*bei shi lu* 備實錄). An omen was no use if not publicized!

Taizu knew the value of propaganda very well, even while he dismissed the ministers' words as "pretty speeches." He himself promulgated fantastic stories suggesting that he was destined for greatness from birth, and his writings frequently mentioned signs of Heaven's approval. But because he insisted, as historian Hok-lam Chan has explained, on having "a complete monopoly of such propaganda," he sometimes rejected putative auspicious omens, even punishing those who submitted them.[15] In August of 1372, shortly after the melon incident, Taizu expressed his fear that officials could deceive and manipulate him, as they had done earlier rulers, by inventing and reporting good omens and hiding bad ones. Whereas some earlier emperors had actively encouraged the presentation of good omens, Taizu now ordered Wang Guangyang to permit the presentation only of ill omens, portents of disaster. Six months later, Wang was removed from court.[16] His flattery in the matter of the melons had apparently backfired. Wang's political misfortune may explain why the *Veritable Records* make Tao Kai the spokesman, whereas Song's eye-witness account featured Wang's analysis. To glorify Taizu and by reflection his son the Yongle emperor, *Veritable Records* compiler Xie Jin may have been trying to glide over the ugly politics of the first Ming reign. For the plain fact is that Taizu ultimately executed almost all of the officials at the 1372 melon audience, men who had worked with him for a long time.

Chen Ning 陳寧, for instance, had been a minor Yuan official and had advised Taizu about combining concern for the people's subsistence with military conquest. In 1372, Chen was high up in the Censorate, the watchdog agency. In 1380, he was sentenced to death for conspiracy with Grand Councilor Hu Weiyong 胡惟庸, whom Taizu believed had plotted a *coup d'etat*. Zhao Yong 趙庸 had commanded troops for Taizu since 1361, and Taizu had ennobled him as a marquis; in 1393, he was executed on charges of conspiring with another long-time comrade of the emperor. Grand Councilor Wang Guangyang, who had been honored as the "loyal and diligent earl," was forced to commit suicide in 1380. Song Lian died on the road to exile in 1381, after advising and serving Taizu for over two decades.[17] Of the men present at the 1372 audience, only Tao Kai and Mu Ying 沐英, a foster son of Taizu and a successful general, survived Taizu's attacks on the men who had helped him win and hold the throne. Compiler Xie Jin was well aware of this unhappy history. As a brash young man he had himself remonstrated with Taizu: "Your Majesty has grown angry and pulled out roots, cut tendrils, and executed evil traitors. . . . Some people in the morning are esteemed, and in the evening they are executed."[18] Two decades later, Xie may have assigned the speaking role to Tao Kai to avoid raising the names of this unfortunate cadre of advisers when writing of an omen intended to symbolize the benevolent rule of his patron's father.

The evidence that any of these men actually plotted against Taizu is slim, and in any case no plot could justify Taizu's execution of tens of thousands of alleged co-conspirators, whom he ferreted out, or implicated, in a process that came to be known as assigning "melon-vine guilt."[19] But if we look closely at what was said in the 1372 melon audience and at what was happening at that time, it seems likely that the ministers were, in fact, trying to manipulate Taizu, just as he suspected. Let us return to the rather strange series of utterances at the beginning of the presentation of the melons. Tao Kai, according to the *Veritable Records*, said:

> "Your Majesty is ruling. Melons sharing a stalk have been produced in Jurong. Jurong is Your Majesty's ancestral home. This is really a good omen."[20]

Taizu's essay reports in less stately language that the ministers said:

> "Now, when Your Majesty is ruling, melons growing from the same stalk have been produced in Jurong. Well, Jurong is the emperor's ancestral home. It goes without saying that this is a good omen!"

Why the emphasis on Jurong county? Since Taizu was the emperor, an auspicious omen anywhere in Ming territory could have been considered to apply to him. Moreover, it seems very odd to have to remind someone of the location of his own ancestral home. That Song Lian omits this comment from his account emphasizes its apparent superfluity. What could it mean?

Jurong county, close by the early Ming capital of Nanjing where the conversation was taking place, had indeed been the home of Taizu's ancestors.[21] Yet Taizu himself had been born north of the Yangzi River, in Fengyang, and he considered that his home town.[22] Following Han imperial precedent, he permanently exempted Fengyang residents from taxes and labor service, and at the time of the melon incident he was constructing a lavish capital city there called Zhongdu ("Middle Capital"). Some officials disapproved of the choice of the location for a new capital. The place was backward, and poor, and isolated. By the time of the melon audience in 1372, building Zhongdu was already costing huge amounts of money and many laborers' lives.[23] In 1375, long-time adviser Liu Ji 劉基 (1311–1375) wrote that even though Fengyang was the emperor's home, it was not fit to rule from. So Taizu finally agreed to keep Nanjing as his main capital: a capital of past regimes, located right on the great Yangzi River in what a Portuguese visitor later called "a very fertile, fresh and beautiful country."[24] (In 1420, the Yongle emperor made Beijing (Peking) into the main capital of the Ming dynasty, keeping Nanjing as a secondary capital.) I think that in 1372, the Jurong origin of the double melons was stressed specifically to push Taizu toward this change in policy, to convince him to abandon the Zhongdu project and choose Nanjing as his permanent capital. There was no need whatsoever, based on historical precedent, to select the dynastic founder's home town as the capital. But seeing Taizu's heart set on selecting a hometown capital, the ministers may have proposed Jurong as an alternate home town, making next-door Nanjing a natural choice for the capital. They were using the melon omen to change Taizu's mind in a current policy debate.

Furthermore, Song Lian may have been intervening in a second policy debate. For Song's preface and hymn not only reported what others had said, but also voiced his own considered views on what the melons meant. Song's hymn of praise says:

> In the fields of Jurong
> beings are without blemish.
> Divine melons show forth:
> different fruits, same stem.
> The melons did not ripen singly,
> but grew together.
> The two *qis* [i.e., yin and yang energy] nourished matter;
> twin stars descended in spirit.
> Their hidden chambers both sweet,
> icy jades competing in loveliness.
> Bright moons, double wheels—
> it seems they can stand up to the comparison!

Song does begin with the fields of Jurong, but the locality recedes, and the melons, the other part of the equation, come into focus in a long, lush description. Song argues that they refer to conditions in the whole newly conquered and still expanding empire. His prose argument begins: "The August Ming sets the pattern for the nine regions [of China]; its virtue soaks, its benevolence covers. Harmonious airs rise fragrantly, and numinous beings signal prosperity." Song then refers to the melon plants as representing the spread of the Chinese people, based on the orthodox interpretation of a song from the classic *Book of Songs* (see Chapter 6). But he moves quickly to a more specific interpretation. Melons become a symbol of empire, of conquest.

> I pray that, as these melons
> cooperate in auspiciousness and join in blessing,
> there will also be peace in China,
> growing until the azure [sky] is its cover.

—that is, until the Ming empire encompasses the whole world. "What is the message?" Song's hymn asks, and he replies:

The border areas will unbrokenly extend,
the four regions will yield,
and virtue will move in the eight directions.[25]

Melons may have particularly appealed to Song Lian as a metaphor for a united Ming empire. It was the duty of each new dynasty to write the history of the one before it, and in presenting the *Yuan History* to Ming Taizu in 1370, he and other compilers (including Tao Kai) had written of China in the late Yuan period as having been "divided up like a melon."[26] Now it was whole again.

Yet Song's interpretation is even more specific than this. He refers to the regional origin of melons in the Northwest, where the desert haven of Turfan, irrigated with snowmelt from distant mountains running through underground tunnels, was justly famed for its melons (and is still today).

> Now, melons appeared originally among the Uighur people. China subdued [that region] and obtained [melons], so they are called "Western." Today, the emperor has ordered the great generals to march west to Gansu and Xiliang. . . . the Western regions all with one heart come to the court, shoulder to shoulder submitting tribute. That Heaven manifests matching good omens, is it not also because of this?[27]

The melons, then, specifically have to do with Ming campaigns in the Northwest. The Gansu corridor had been conquered two years earlier, and just that summer of 1372 Ming troops had fought and raided as far as Jiayuguan and Dunhuang. Yet Mongol victories in the West during the same summer would lead Taizu, early in 1373, to give up the goal of conquering Outer Mongolia.[28] Song's comments, seen in this immediate context, may not only be celebrating the Gansu victories, but also arguing for continuation of a policy to press further north.

The two agendas the ministers appear to have pursued by presenting and discussing the double melons both focus on the emperor, but they address two different spatial aspects of the empire. Tao Kai and Wang Guangyang locate empire at court and seek to place Taizu in a proper center, a capital whose maintenance would not drain away resources, a capital well established by the patronage of several earlier dynasties. Jurong is important to them as a place close enough to this capital to stand in for it, and they appeal to the emperor on the basis of its being his ancestral home. Song Lian's interpretation looks instead at the court's outward reach. Answering a question the other interpretation does not address—Why melons?—he uses the history of melons to stress a connection between the Chinese heartland and distant western areas that have just been re-incorporated. Taizu's status as conqueror and universal ruler, rather than his origins as a Jurong man, is the point.

Taizu did tend toward paranoia. As Edward Farmer points out, his vigilance and alertness were what had made him "the sole survivor of a prolonged period of dog-eat-dog competition that destroyed all of his rivals."[29] Late in life he instructed his descendants, "If you take your safety for granted and forget to take precautions, then evil persons will be able to plot. Neither your life nor your state can be protected. You must be prepared day and night as if you were going into battle."[30] Yet it is unfair to attribute to Taizu's incipient paranoia his fear that his advisers were using omens to manipulate him. The ministers were acting within a long tradition of court politics in which, as Rafe de Crespigny has perceptively suggested, warning portents and auspicious omens "were used by both the emperor and his officials as a means of conducting debate at one remove, and also of generating propaganda for their respective positions among a wider public opinion."[31] The ministers showed Taizu the melons, and their texts showed readers the emperor receiving the melons from their hands and accompanied by their words. On the one hand, this presentation flattered the emperor and contributed to dynastic propaganda. But on the other hand, it also allowed ministers to use the melons—the voice of Heaven speaking to the Son of Heaven—to influence Taizu and shape policy without having to disagree openly.

Beyond addressing the immediate policy issues, the scholar-officials were making a claim to interpretive authority: a claim that they were qualified to mediate between Heaven and the emperor.[32] This role Taizu was determined to deny them. Taizu told his descendants that they should take strange occurrences like misplaced objects or a sick horse as signs that danger lurked. But he instructed them that rather than relying on expert diviners,

> you shall carefully make the decision yourself. . . . If there
> is a fierce wind or a sudden thunder coming directly
> against you, or if there is a bird in flight or beast afoot

approaching strangely, this is a warning from the spirits. . . . Celestial phenomena cannot be caused by man; the others are all things that can be caused by man. Perhaps evil persons would take advantage by making it look like there was something when there was not.[33]

Rather than setting aside the double melons entirely, Taizu thought carefully about their meaning. Against the ministers' claims he defended his prerogative of interpretation with a barrage of self-contradictory arguments. Let us turn to his side of the story.

Chapter II

What the Emperor Said

Fruit and melons without land won't grow;
fish and dragons without water can't function.

Su Shi

Taizu's own preface to his ode on the melon audience reports that he was astonished and puzzled when he first saw the melons, even a bit peeved to be interrupted at work. Song Lian, by contrast, paints a picture of a pleased sovereign who first modestly refuses and then respectfully accepts the auspicious omen. To Song Lian's eyes, "the emperor appeared gratified" upon seeing the melons. Before asking about historical precedents, "he looked at them again and again for a long time." And after hearing Wang Guangyang's recitation of precedents, he "modestly hung back and would not agree." Song Lian also reports that the emperor to some degree accepted the argument that the melons were numinous—filled with spiritual energy and meaning.

> The emperor said, "Ah!
> We are still dissatisfied [with the ministers' explanation].
> Good omens ought to lie in *people;*
> how can *things* transmit them?
> [But] *if* things are blessed,
> it is proper to offer them in the imperial ancestral temple,
> since it is my ancestors'
> accumulated blessings that they show."
> Not boasting of the ripe melons,
> the emperor thus did not keep them,
> but only personally expressed this thought:
> "My common followers
> respond to Heaven with fruit [or, "really respond to Heaven"]:
> this is flourishing virtue."

With respect to the ancestral offering, Song's preface explains:

14

[The emperor] would not agree [to Wang's interpretation] but presently considered that, since the numinous gift had reached him, he could not refuse to accept it. Then he ordered a eunuch to put them [the melons] in the Qianqing Palace. The next day, he offered them in the imperial ancestral temple.[1]

Of the many comments Taizu made on the melons, Song selected those that made the emperor seem an earnest ruler, appropriately humble before Heaven, and concerned chiefly with virtue and human affairs. Modestly accepting reflected glory, the emperor presents the choice tribute to his ancestors, saying that it was their virtue, if anything, that called forth the omen. The account had to preserve some of what Taizu actually said, since it was written for him. Yet his utterances are put in the best possible light. Song's prose preface gives none of the many complex arguments Taizu made, which we will see below, and his hymn reports only the emperor's view that it is the honesty and hard work of the people that is the real good omen. Song had long tutored Taizu in aspects of rulership. Perhaps in this piece he was trying to teach his sovereign how he *ought* to have behaved, and spoken, and thought about the omen.

Yet there was more to Taizu's response than "becoming" imperial modesty. First of all, it was unnecessary for a ruler to make a show of rejecting omens. The Han emperor Wu (Wudi; r. 141–87 B.C.), for instance, liked omens so well that he once accepted two contradictory interpretations of an omen, generously rewarding both interpreters.[2] Lucky omens had usually been especially welcome early in a dynasty, when a new ruling house "still had to fight for final recognition."[3] Taizu's reluctance set a new precedent, which his successors observed into the sixteenth century. Second, despite all the talk about achieving perfect sagely rule, the Ming government in fact confronted a panoply of serious problems in 1372: border wars; rebellions among Han and minority people; piracy and invasions from the sea; and famine, flood, drought, pestilence, and locust plagues in various parts of the empire. Taizu and his government had successfully dealt with many of the problems. Yes, tribute missions were coming in from overseas, demonstrating the magnetism of the new emperor's virtue—and of China's goods and markets. Yes, reconstruction and unification were proceeding. But it was quite reasonable for Taizu to worry that his throne was not perfectly secure and to feel that complacency was unwarranted, even dangerous. Contrary to Song Lian's wishful presentation, then, the emperor was not merely being modest in rejecting the melons as an omen his virtue had brought forth. Rather, in accord with Hok-lam Chan's observation, he was asserting his unique right to accept or reject phenomena as omens, and to interpret them. He claimed that prerogative in a number of odd and conflicting statements, reported differently in the three primary accounts.[4]

Once Taizu had recovered from his initial surprise, and following the explanation that the melons grew in Jurong, he first alluded to the antique ritual classic *Record of Rites*. He may not have done so in the audience itself; Song Lian does not report it. But by the time he wrote the essay, he had had time to look up a classical quotation that served his purpose nicely: "Heaven's *qi* descends; Earth's *qi* rises up." Upon hearing or reading these lines, every scholar would have known instantly that the *Record of Rites* itself continues: "Heaven and Earth are in harmonious cooperation; all things bud and grow."[5]

It was important that Taizu embellish his thoughts with a quotation, for education justified status and power. The social and political elite of China were highly educated. From the Song period on, they rarely held office by hereditary right, but instead had to pass rigorous civil service examinations on the classics, Confucian writings, history, poetry, and policy. Early in his reign Taizu had re-instituted the examinations, but in 1373, the year after the melon audience, he would suspend the exams for a decade, because he distrusted the literati men the examination process favored. By 1470, however, the examinations had become essentially the only route into office, and a very important part of social and cultural life.[6] The elite gentry class, with family traditions of learning, and with land-holdings or mercantile capital that assured young men leisure to study, naturally did best in the exams. But printed books to study from were readily bought, and commoners who studied hard could pass the three-tiered examinations, win an official post, and rise into the gentry class, earning tax exemptions and other privileges related to newly acquired status. Conversely, gentry families whose boys balked at spending long years poring over old books could lose their elite status and their access to political office (girls were excluded from the exams, but not necessarily from education). So, education was in itself a status marker. A poor orphan, Taizu had learned to read and write only as an adult, and although he spent his days reading memorials and writing edicts, admonitions, essays, and even poems, he remained insecure about his classical training. He wanted to demonstrate his mastery of the classics with this allusion.

He continues in his own words that he has heard of "auspicious grain, double water lilies, 'rejoicing-union' flowers, trees that grow together, and two heads of grain on one stem. [But] produce on the same [melon] stalk I have never heard of nor seen. So I greatly wondered at it." Taizu admits that there have been plant omens in the past, but not double melons. He is contradicting Wang Guangyang's report on the Han-era double melons and Han Yu's memorial, but since Taizu and Song Lian report opposite sides of the conversation in two different texts, it is impossible to know who spoke first. Was Wang correcting his sovereign, or was Taizu dismissing the learned scholar's evidence?

As he did in many of his edicts, Taizu then refers to his own life experience.

> Moreover, I come from a farming family. I personally tilled the ditch-drained fields. Yearly I saw the five grains grow and develop, but I never heard of [melons] sharing a stalk! I lived among the group of heroes for eleven years, and as king and emperor have already recorded ten years. [Yet] I have never heard of this [type of] good omen! Because I am not familiar with the *Odes* and *Documents*, I lack a broad view of antiquity and modern times—that must be why.[7]

How shall we interpret that last sentence? Is it modesty? It sounds like crude sarcasm. Elsewhere Taizu wrote scornfully of scholars "who sit looking on in the market and the village, bragging of their own ability, enjoying flattery from the ordinary people[.] When did they ever experience or witness anything? . . . They merely spouted empty rhetoric, thinking it ability, but making no contribution to affairs."[8] Taizu's sarcastic comment in the melon essay about his own lack of book learning points up his mistrust of scholars. Taizu emphasizes instead the value of the practical knowledge he has gained as farmer, soldier, and ruler. "Where does knowledge lie?" he seems to ask: "in books or in the school of hard knocks?"

In this passage, Taizu seems to deny that double melons even exist. But later in the essay, he interrupts his last argument to question the existence of folk-tale fruits like the double pear and fiery jujube—divine fruits ensuring immortality—and the fairy peach, which blooms once every three thousand years in the orchard of the Queen Mother of the West, a mythological deity popular in Tang poetry, Daoism, and popular religion. Taizu calls these fruits "of which one hears, but which one cannot see."[9] But these double melons are there, right before his eyes. Why is he reluctant to accept them?

Song Lian interprets his reluctance as modesty, and that is, indeed, the next pose Taizu strikes in his own account.

> At the time when I was presented with the melons, the group of officials took their virtue as redounding to me [*de gui yu zhen* 德歸於朕]. When I listened to their speeches, I felt anxious and ashamed. I don't presume to call forth omens with my virtue but only pray for the harvest to be abundant and the people happy."

But is this real modesty? Taizu continues: "I fundamentally am of slight virtue, but even if I had virtue, the Lord-on-high [*Shangdi* 上帝] could not respond with a good omen to make me arrogant. [On the other hand,] if I committed a slight transgression, He would surely announce it with a bad sign to make me careful about my person, and not let the people reach the point of calamity."[10] Here, as in many of his other writings, Taizu assumes that he is in communication with, as he puts it, the Lord-on-high.[11] It was to this deity that he had sacrificed in late 1367, asking for good weather as a sign that he should take the throne.[12] Now that he is emperor his virtue is so crucial, Taizu suggests, that Lord-on-high would warn him even about his minor faults but would not risk his becoming arrogant by congratulating him on his successes. That is hardly a modest stance; rather, it reflects the sense of his own centrality. A few years later, Taizu would express his centrality in ritual terms by uniting what had been separate sacrifices to Heaven and Earth. The unified ceremony, described by a recent historian as "a microcosmic re-creation of the universe in which all natural forces and deities headed by heaven and earth . . . held the annual meeting," emphasized the emperor's pivotal position in the universe as the mediator of that meeting.[13]

Taizu's peculiar claim that Lord-on-high might chastise but would never praise him seems to foreclose the possibility of any good omen at all: a radical revision to traditional political theory. The passage is dramatically different in the *Veritable Records* version:

> The emperor said: "Auspicious vegetable omens, like auspicious grain, double water lilies, 'rejoicing-union' flowers, and melons on the same stalk—these are all examples. The ministers take their virtue as redounding to me. I am not virtuous and dare not presume [*bugandang* 不敢當]. Even if I had virtue, Heaven [*Tian* 天] would not express it through an auspicious sign of one creature. If I committed a slight transgression, [Heaven] would surely use signs to reprimand and warn me, to make me careful about my person, and to protect the people from getting to the point of calamity."[14]

As well as changing the name of the deity from Lord-on-high to the less personal Heaven, Xie Jin, the compiler of the *Veritable Records*, has transformed Taizu's claim—that his virtue would not call forth omens—into a conventional phrase of polite modesty, appropriate to conversation but not true to Taizu's report of his thoughts. An emperor should be modest, but should not deprecate himself too convincingly.[15] Xie further dilutes Taizu's expressions by removing the word "bad" from the description of the sign Heaven would provide to warn the emperor about his faults. Xie's account even goes so far as to completely reverse Taizu's argument in one way: part of the same list of vegetable omens cited above appears, with one minor difference in wording, but now the emperor accepts the melons as canonical. Xie's changes have the effect of dampening the emperor's disagreement with his ministers' view that these particular melons were a message about him from Heaven. That disagreement is reduced to one final point.

This final point is a most interesting argument, which the *Veritable Records* presents accurately, but briefly. The emperor said: "These vegetable omens are produced in that ground and only respond to the people of that ground. What does it have to do with me? If throughout the space between heaven and earth times are peaceful and harvests rich, *that* is the omen of king rule. So kingly omens do not appear in trivial things."[16] How, in other words, could the cosmically significant state of the empire be expressed by a couple of honeydews? As Wolfram Eberhard hypothesizes in discussing ill omens, if the assumption was that human actions or qualities could be reflected in natural anomalies, "the size of the portents should, in a hierarchical society such as the Chinese, be found to be in relation to the status of the person(s) who caused it."[17]

Taizu's own essay presents this argument more fully, in his usual run-on style. He writes, and may have said in the original audience:

> In antiquity and today, the auspicious signs of the five grains and the lucky omens of vegetation have roots nourished in rich soil. Any omens or blessings that come from the products of a piece of land not bigger than several feet or tens of inches or so must redound to the one who owns and manages [the land]. It has nothing to do with me! . . . Whatever five-grains or vegetable lucky omens arise within a piece of land of several feet, several tens of inches, or several Chinese acres (*mou*), they only congratulate him who owns and manages it! If throughout the space between heaven and earth the times are peaceful and the harvest abundant, *that* is the sign of kingly rule. Kingly omens do not exist among trivialities![18]

Song Lian's hymn, quoted at the beginning of this chapter, gives a faulty echo of this argument when the emperor says: "Good omens ought to lie in *people*; how can *things* transmit them?" The omission of the term "trivial" in this summary helps neutralize Taizu's skepticism about whether the melons are truly an omen. Song portrays an emperor who, quite properly, values people rather than things. Taizu's point was quite different: that kingly omens appear only in large-scale phenomena. He claims a distinct authority for the monarch: his special relation with Lord-on-high (or Heaven) means that the emperor's virtue or vice uniquely affects the peace and prosperity of the whole world, but is too great to be reflected in silly little things like melons.

But while rejecting the significance of local omens as messages to or about himself, Taizu accepts that vegetable omens do signify something. He acknowledges a very local moral authority: Heaven uses vegetable omens to commend even farmers for their virtue. From Taizu's perspective, imperial authority, insofar as it springs from the moral approbation of Heaven, is different from the moral worth of a farmer in scope, but not in kind. The theme of the farmer's virtue continues in Taizu's ode, dedicated to the paired deities Heaven and Earth.

> Heaven is a marvelous mirror;
> the gods of Earth tally.
> They know that my good people
> work hard at farming from morning until night.

What do vegetable omens respond to? The hard work of the farmers, is the answer given here. Tao Kai, Wang Guangyang quoting Han Yu, and Song Lian all expressed confidence that the appearance of the auspicious melons signified that the virtue of the Ming founder was permeating the country and bringing forth good *qi* and numinous plants. By contrast, Taizu's arguments do not make his own role clear. It may be that his pacification of the realm has made it possible for farmers to cultivate the land in peace, but Taizu does not say that. His ode continues with a reference to the *Record of Rites* verse he invoked in the preface:

> Heaven's *qi* descends;
> Earth's *qi* rises up.
> The yellow springs and the fertile earth
> take shape together.
> From the same stalk double produce
> came from Jurong.
> The commoner did not eat it himself,
> but with sunburned back came to the court.

The good omen is not attributed so much to the production of the melons as it is to the selfless travail of the farmer who, upon identifying the fruits as auspicious, took them to the imperial court to share the good sign with his sovereign and acknowledge that the good omen could only have resulted from the emperor's great virtue. Taizu describes the melons:

> Blue-green clouds of many colors,
> partly like emerald, partly like coral.
> I split them and drink the juice—
> Crossing Chu, eating duckweed.

This makes it sound as though Taizu unceremoniously ate the melons. But according to Song's report, the emperor first offered them up in the imperial ancestral temple. Taizu may have omitted that because admitting that he had elevated the melons to the status of a sacrifice to his ancestors would have run counter to the suspicious tone that dominates his essay. Nonetheless, he does mitigate his negative stance by describing the melons as delicious and beautiful, and by alluding to a legendary incident that took place near Nanjing in the distant past. The King of Chu saw huge red fruits growing from plants along the river, and Confucius explained that these fruits were auspicious. Any reader would immediately have thought of this incident and understood that Taizu was praising the melons as being like these mythical, magical fruits. Despite his arguments to the contrary, Taizu accepted the melons as significant to himself—significant enough to offer up to his ancestors, to praise, and to record.

Rationalist Confucian scholars sometimes argued that omens were not mystical communications from Heaven but should be studied as "useful barometers of social sentiment and public virtue."[19] Taizu accords with this kind of interpretation by returning to the theme that it is the subject's diligence and loyalty that are truly the good omen. His ode concludes with congratulations and blessings for the melon grower.

> The commoner's heart is filial and obedient.
> How could I have any ability?
> Clumsily I utter a few phrases
> to praise the sincerity of the commoner.
> I wish you in every generation
> a harmonious family and a peaceful home,[20]
> and determined sons and grandsons
> [like] enfeoffed lords [or] ranked dukes.
> Be it for a thousand or ten thousand years,
> do not forget to work at farming.

Taizu's final good wish for the farmer, that his family will prosper and spread, reminds us of Song Lian's likening the spreading melon plant of the classic *Book of Songs* to the flourishing of the dynasty. The spread of the empire, of the ruler's authority, depends on the increase and continuance not only of his own family, but of the families of diligent and virtuous subjects. The farmer seems more a symbol here than a real person. Taizu's reference to nobility is symbolic, too: the descendants will be numerous and fine, but they will also stick to farming. Taizu takes the opportunity of the ode to emphasize a theme of his social vision, that every man should follow his father's profession, and not think about moving up. Taizu also gave the farmer a small amount of money: 1,200 copper cash.[21] That was not much, but an imperial ode was surely enough to make the farmer a celebrity back home. The reader of any of the three accounts might well assume that he lived happily every after. But we will see that he was not so lucky.

The three primary accounts of the melon audience use the incident differently. Taizu paints the officials as a credulous and sycophantic crowd from whom he distances himself to maintain his independence of mind. While he allows complexities or contradictions in his own thinking to come through clearly, he shortens and manipulates the officials' utterances in order to dismiss them, expressing disdain for men set all a-flutter by some fruit. He simultaneously accepts and rejects the melons as an auspicious omen and presents a number of arguments about them that go far beyond expressing the modesty Song Lian uses to justify Taizu's puzzling reaction. Taizu disputes scholar Wang Guangyang's historical evidence for prior examples of auspicious melons. He argues that Lord-on-high would warn him about his transgressions, but would not stoop to commend him through so trivial a thing as a piece of fruit.

Taizu further postulates that each farmer has a legitimate sphere of influence in the sense that the appearance of lucky produce within a field or garden may show Heaven and Earth responding to the farmer's own virtue. Taizu's policies on local governance went through various phases. In this early stage in which the melon incident occurred, a time when the Ming bureaucracy was just establishing control, Taizu allowed existing social authorities in small spheres to remain in place. He honored local deities and locally respected men, to help build dynastic strength out of existing social relationships.[22] The idea that a farmer's virtue could call forth auspicious omens on his own land made sense to Taizu in this phase, and was certainly preferable to granting that scholar-officials had the knowledge and moral authority to judge and interpret such omens for him. Despite his apparent rejection of the melon omen, then, Taizu did use it as propaganda: to assert his superiority to his court officials, to tout his concern for the farming people, and to highlight his special relationship to Heaven—all central themes of his rule.

Ming Taizu truncated the ministerial utterances and gave space to his own thoughts in his preface and ode. The later *Veritable Records*, based on a third, lost, contemporary record of the conversation, pares down Taizu's rambling rant and allows the ministers to state their case more fully. The account presents two dignified characters: an earnest emperor and a learned official. The emperor agrees with the official on many points but has one rational, even laudable argument against accepting fruit as a significant communication from an impersonal Heaven to a powerful ruler: it simply is not weighty enough. The creation of both of these characters fits in with the intentions of compiler Xie Jin. In his youth Xie had severely criticized some of the Ming founder's policies, including punishing evil-doers with executions "spreading like a vine," and had even remonstrated with him about his habit of fashioning supernatural tales about himself.[23] But for some reason, Taizu, though displeased, had only banished Xie from the court, and Xie survived to craft a most favorable portrait of him, writing elsewhere:

> Hail the Great Ming Grand Progenitor, the Holy and Divine, Cultivated and Martial, Revered and Brilliant, Dynasty-founding, Refined and Virtuous, Successful and Accomplished, One-with-Heaven, and the Great Filial Exalted Emperor! He responded to the auspicious cycle of fortune of a thousand years and the accumulated achievements of the multitude of sages. With profound tenderness of the Mandate of Heaven, he arose by treading in steps unsupported by [the wealth of] a single foot of land. People joyfully rallied to him and faithfully rendered service; in less than three years he had already ensconced himself at the national capital. 'When the Dragon flies, the clouds follow.' The land of Hua Xia [i.e., Han Chinese] as well as the Man and Diao [i.e., non-Han tribes of the south and north] all but follow and submit. The sun shines and the moon overlooks, and the mountains, the streams, the ominous as well as the auspicious all rest in peace.[24]

Such exaggerated language was intended to exalt both Ming Taizu and Xie Jin's boss, Yongle, who had usurped the throne from his eldest brother's son in a bloody civil war. Yongle justified his violent reversal of his father's choice of successor by saying that he was protecting his father's institutional legacy. Omens were a mode of legitimation that Yongle liked, and his father's melons also reflected glory on him. On the other hand, Xie also portrayed the ministers as dignified partners in government, perhaps to influence the Yongle emperor to treat officials—like himself—respectfully.[26] In this he ultimately failed: he antagonized Yongle and died in prison.[27]

In the third account, written immediately after the melon audience, Song Lian addresses the Ming founder himself. The text's intimate purpose is signaled by, among other things, the absence of surnames from the long list of those present at the time the melons were presented. Yet Song's text also propagandizes the Ming enterprise both to the educated public and to posterity. Song reduces all of Taizu's convoluted arguments to a modest reluctance. He leaves out Taizu's ambivalent pride in his farming origins and his uneasy reference to his education; he leaves out Taizu's certainty that Lord-on-high would let him know if he erred even slightly; he leaves out the assertion that kingly virtue does not appear in anything so trivial as melons; he leaves out too the notion that the farmer's virtue calls forth his own omens on his own land; and he leaves out the deep suspicion of scholar-officials that comes across so clearly in Taizu's version. Instead, lavishly congratulating his protégé, the emperor, on his successes as evinced by the melons, Song Lian simultaneously flatters him, instructs him in the proper posture for an emperor presented with such signs, and suggests to other readers that Taizu has already learned that posture.

All of the ministers took what Robert Campany calls the "locative approach," discussed in the Introduction. Double melons mean something about the Ming center and its control outward, the ministers assert. Yet just as Taizu's own writings exhibit pessimism about his ability to project virtue outward from the throne, his response to the melons also suggests a world view closer to an "anti-locative" cosmography, one that eschews carefully centered hierarchy and blurs distinctions between inner and outer.[28] In his essay on the double melons, Taizu indeed insists that he is critical to the health of the cosmos, but he is not just a sacred place-holder. He narrates his own individual story and defines himself as a man who has seen life, has worked like the melon farmer, has fought, and has studied. He seems less concerned than the ministers to display each and every product in terms of its relation to the imperial position. His lists of fairy fruits are random, not ordered in a neat hierarchy or system. Individual virtue, whether his own or that of a local farmer, may call forth responsive signs independently. Taizu does finally domesticate the melon farmer into the imperial order by noting his obedience in submitting the melons to court, and by offering the melons to his ancestors. But along the way, he has argued that family farms are centers of virtue unto themselves, centers that may produce their own meanings independent of the court. That argument forces the historian to consider the fact that before the melons could be deployed at court, they had to arrive there. How did that happen?

Chapter III

Up from the Garden

The Ming empire was administratively divided into thirteen provinces, nine more loosely controlled defense areas, and two metropolitan areas the size of provinces. Within those were units called prefectures, which had a longer history, and below those again were the subprefectures and counties. The metropolitan area of Nanzhili was about the size of Great Britain or Minnesota, with a population of approximately ten million. Yingtian ("Respond to Heaven") prefecture encompassed both the capital city of Nanjing and Jurong county. Jurong county, with its seat at Jurong city and 426 rural villages, had about 206,000 people in the early Ming period,[1] about five times the population of contemporary London. It had one magistrate who had a small staff that helped him in collecting taxes, settling lawsuits, solving crimes, and keeping the peace. The magistrate and the prefect managed the many exchanges between court and locality.

On the day before the audience in 1372, Song Lian reports, Zhang Yulin 張遇林, the prefect of Yingtian, had placed the melons in a plain box, painted a picture or diagram of them on the outside, and asked the Ministry of Rites to present them to the emperor. We do not know how or whether the prefect explained the melons, and we can only guess at his motive in presenting them to Taizu.[2] Perhaps he was expressing Yingtian prefecture's gratitude for a tax exemption bestowed at the request of officials in April of the same year,[3] or perhaps he was angling for a promotion. But in any case, the Yingtian prefectural office was in the capital itself, not in neighboring Jurong county. How did Zhang Yulin get the melons? Taizu's ode says that "the commoner . . . with sunburned back came to the court." Unless this is just poetic invention, the farmer had traveled to Nanjing himself, skipping the intermediate level of the magistrate, and carried the melons to Prefect Zhang's office.

In both locative and anti-locative cosmographies as Robert Campany discusses them, it is the state collector at the center who takes the active role in identifying and interpreting anomalies.[4] Yet on this occasion in 1372, the ministers' use of the melons as flattery, as propaganda, or as intervention in policy debates was premised on the commoner's having brought them to court. Taizu's argument that the moral authority exemplified by the melons accrued to the farmer himself was only possible because the farmer had disagreed. If the Jurong man had not thought the melons referred to the emperor, they would have remained in Jurong.

In creating meaning out of life, people have to decide what to interpret. The world is full of odd things, not all of which were understood to be omens. Melons were specifically protected from theft in Ming law, and were important enough in market garden Jurong that their theft came to carry a penalty of 2 taels of silver, but they are, after all, small things.[5] They do not fit into Michael Loewe's definition of omens as "portents of nature that are obvious to all, and that are of sufficient size and strength to demand explanation," like an eclipse.[6] So in 1372, there had to be a local decision in Jurong, first, that the melons constituted an auspicious anomaly, and second, that they referred to the Ming emperor. Several elements, I believe, entered into this decision: Jurong's standing as a Daoist center, an earlier offering to Ming Taizu, local traditions of understanding odd plants, local relations with magistrates past and present, and the family of the farmer himself.

Just as Nanjing constituted the central place of the early Ming cosmic regime, Jurong was a center of Daoism. A thousand years earlier, the scholar and Daoist Ge Hong had lived in Jurong, and Mount Mao, where three brothers had gathered medicine for the local people, had been the site of a new Daoist revelation. Daoism, with roots in antiquity, included volumes and volumes of scriptures with texts ranging from esoteric discussions of the spiritual to protoscientific treatments of astronomy and the natural world. Text and nature were never far apart: some Jurong Daoists stored scriptures in gourds[7] (called gua 瓜, the same word as used for melons), perhaps because of the primal chaos and fertility signaled by their myriad seeds, perhaps because of the metaphorical connection to the constellation Big Dipper, which was a Daoist deity.

Such gourds were literally full of meaning, but other plants were meaningful too. Pine resin and fungus, for instance, promised purification, long life, and special powers like flight if one subsisted on them instead of grain and meat while carrying out spiritual exercises. In this way of thinking, food and medicine were not clearly distinguished: a discussion of the different kinds of melons (*gua*) for instance, says that green melons plucked in the seventh month are used in many prescriptions, that pumpkin (southern *gua*) and another fruit, northern *gua*, will dispel pain and sickness, and that watermelon (western *gua*) will expel summer heat.[8] Daoists not only ate carefully, but compounded elixirs and pills. In a story relayed by Ming Taizu himself, his mother was said to have been given a fragrant white-powder pellet by a mysterious Daoist on the day before his birth.[9] Not all Daoist medicines were benign, however. Even people who were not full-time spiritual seekers ingested odd substances like arsenic and lead: Daoist elixirs killed two of Ming Taizu's sons.[10] Jurong, perhaps because of its Daoist heritage, had its own long tradition of producing anomolous flora. The county gazetteer lists among local products five kinds of magic fungus and reports a local saying: "The magic fungus is a numinous being; one may encounter it, but one cannot seek it."[11] The celebration and interpretation of odd plants was not unique to Jurong, but it was taken very seriously there.[12]

The 1372 melons were not the first auspicious flora the county had presented to Taizu. In 1355, the emperor-to-be had crossed the Yangzi river from his base to the north in a dramatic maneuver to which he frequently referred, and seized control of the area that included Nanjing and Jurong. As a leader who proclaimed himself a man of the people, Taizu may have seemed approachable, and the counties near Nanjing courted his favor. In April or May 1367, Taizu proclaimed to the subjects of Jurong county:

> From the time I crossed the river, it has been thirteen years, and many auspicious omens from within my territory have come in for presentation. In 1356, grain in Taiping prefecture's Dantu county produced one stem with two heads; in 1357 Yingtian prefecture's Shangyuan county grain produced one stalk with three ears, and Ningguo prefecture's Ningguo county grain produced one stalk with two ears. Today, Jurong county has again presented grain of one stalk with two ears. Now because the subject people are diligent in farming matters, and

are thankful for the harmony of Heaven, it has come to be like this. If you people continue to exert your strength in your ditch-drained fields, in order to serve your parents and teach your wives and sons, you will always be the people of the Great Peace and together enjoy the happiness of a fruitful harvest.[13]

The proclamation agrees with some of Taizu's comments in the later melon audience. Indirectly, Taizu seems willing to take some credit for the omens, but the direct message is clear: auspicious flora come from proper behavior demonstrated by the farming people and are unimportant when compared with the real blessings of peaceful communities, harmonious families, and rich harvests. The proclamation omits any reference to the imperial ancestors' having lived in Jurong, and points out that Jurong's production of auspicious grains is not unique. Perhaps it was intended to dampen enthusiasm for such tribute, and it may have done so, for the proclamation is not included in the 1496 Jurong county gazetteer's collection of imperial orders germane to the county, and it is recorded in the 1750/1900 Jurong gazetteer in only one line.[14]

In addition to the lukewarm proclamation of 1367, there is another reason that the presentation of melons in 1372 is surprising in the local context. Double melons had appeared before and would appear later in Jurong, but they tended to be associated with the county magistrate. Although he usually held office for only three or at most nine years, the magistrate was the key figure in good governance. As one man wrote, reflecting on the landscape of his native place from which he had long been absent:

> I am unsure what changes may have taken place in it. It all depends on the quality of our magistrates. If they have all been good magistrates, who have gained the cooperation of the people and have brought on Heaven's bounty, then the flora and fauna will have flourished even more; the mountains will have become even finer and the waters clearer, and the pleasure of it all will have increased. But this is not what I hear. I fear that what I used to enjoy now looks lamentable, and that the local people must be envying the immortals on their transcendental journey.[15]

If a magistrate collected a reasonable amount of taxes, did not leave too many crimes unsolved or lawsuits unsettled, and escaped rebellion and other serious trouble on his watch, he might be promoted. Some magistrates poured their energy into making things better—by fairly apportioning tax burdens among the rich and poor; building city walls, bridges, altars, schools, orphanages, free pharmacies, and old-age homes; improving popular morality; and destroying popular cults of which they disapproved. Often, from about 1470 onward, such activist magistrates wrote or oversaw the compilation or updating of a local gazetteer, a publication that recorded the county's history and famous inhabitants, its institutions and scenic points of pride, its poetry and its products. Such a gazetteer might be a venue for competition among local gentry families vying for honor, and it might also enhance the magistrate's reputation by recording his activities. The magistrate might also earn a record in the gazetteer for his own native place,—which was always far from any post in which he served, so as to prevent any collusion between the magistrate and the locals that could threaten the dynasty. Yet some cooperation with locals was necessary in order for a magistrate to get anything done. Magistrates hired lower-class men as policemen and literate men as clerks, and they worked with landowners and local gentry families in almost every area of governance. If a magistrate was honest, hardworking, and lucky, or if he had a good relationship with the community or those who dominated it, he might earn a place in a local shrine or signs of Heavenly approval. Several magistrates of Jurong had achieved this kind of success.

Magistrate Zhang Kan 張侃, for instance, was a Song-era magistrate whose good governance, specifically his building of a Buddhist pond into which one released living creatures, had called forth five vegetable omens, including lucky melons (rui gua 瑞瓜) described as "[two] on one stem" (gua bing di 瓜並蒂 or bing di gua). A commemorative inscription, complete with a picture of each omen, had been carved as a stone stele in 1229 to immortalize the omens and Zhang's accomplishments.[16] On the other side of our incident, in the middle of the Ming period, more double melons and lucky vegetables congratulated Jurong magistrates. Local gentryman Wang Shao 王韶, after earning a provincial degree in 1450, had been a proper official whose virtue improved the morality of the people in his jurisdiction. But as he preferred to grow old at home rather than remain in office, he returned to Jurong and spent his days with poetry

Jurong Town. From *Yitai Zhang shi jiasheng* (Genealogy of the Yitai Zhang).

and wine, adopting the name "Man of the Way Who has Returned to Leisure." He helped compile the 1496 county gazetteer and contributed many poems to it, including one that celebrates the double melons and other auspicious signs that appeared under Magistrate Zhang Hui 張蕙 in about 1470, and one celebrating the auspicious grain that grew in response to Magistrate Wang Xi 王僖 in the 1490s. Both of these magistrates were activists, and both had relations with Jurong gentry society; Wang Xi collected materials for the county gazetteer, and Zhang Hui contributed many poems, poems composed over wine, perhaps in the company of Wang Shao himself. Wang Shao's poems conclude with compliments to the dynasty but explain the lucky plants as springing from the good governance of the magistrate. The people, who presumably grew the plants, appear only as grateful subjects, in one poem adding to the celebration with their songs. A third Ming magistrate, Xu Guang 徐廣, called forth auspicious grain and lucky melons in about 1488.[17] It was a Jurong tradition, then, to link double melons with good magistrates rather than with the emperor.

In this county so rich in strange plants and their lore, it is hardly surprising that a pair of double melons was interpreted as an omen in the early Ming period. The Song inscription and picture commemorating Magistrate Zhang Kan's melons were still in the county school—indeed they were there long after the early Ming. The inscription and a schema of the picture were included in a late Qing collection of Jurong county inscriptions that leaves out characters that had become illegible with time, and hence the Song inscription must have been copied from actual steles (texts engraved on stone), not from the text that had been reprinted in the 1496 gazetteer.[18] And in 1847, Jurong County School Instructor Zhang copied the double melons from the inscription into a painting with a short poem; the image of two round melons seemed very appropriate to celebrate his concubine's presenting him with twins.[19] (Double melons decorate at least one popular print of "One Hundred Boys," a lucky image to be pasted up at the New Year.[20]) The inscription must have been there to be seen in the early Ming period by anyone who had occasion to visit the county school.

The man who grew the melons could easily have seen the inscription. Song Lian tells us his name: Zhang Guan. Although Guan's father and grandfather did not hold office, and had probably not even taken the civil service examinations, they were educated men of good family, who lived in or very near Jurong town.[21] Such men would have had occasion to visit the county school. This was part of a government complex found in every county; two sets of buildings housed on one side the county school where students who would take the examinations registered (in the Ming period little actual teaching went on there) and on the other the temple to Confucius and his disciples, where the magistrate carried out regular ceremonies. The complex was the headquarters for ceremonial meetings between local gentry and the magistrate. For instance, there the magistrate might hold the "community libation ceremony," to honor the old and powerful men of the county and be recognized by them in return. Attending any such occasion, the men of the Zhang family would certainly have noticed the Song inscription commemorating an illustrious magistrate who happened to share their surname. In fact, as we will see, the Zhangs had a close connection with the Jurong county school. Zhang Guan surely knew about Zhang Kan's melons.

So when Zhang Guan's garden produced two melons on one stalk, it made sense to him to identify them as a lucky omen. From the central perspective, the perspective of emperor and court, with which historians normally begin, it seems only common sense, too, that those melons would be interpreted as a sign of Heaven's approval of the new Ming emperor. But now that we have examined the local context—Taizu's lack of enthusiasm about Jurong's lucky grain five years before and the Jurong tradition of interpreting such omens as referring to the magistrate—we know enough to think it rather odd that Zhang Guan brought the melons to the capital. He may have chosen to interpret them as referring to the emperor because the incumbent magistrate, Huang Wenwei 黃文蔚, was undistinguished; indeed he left almost no trace. Zhang may have considered him undeserving of Heavenly approbation, yet may have still been reluctant to insult him by passing the melons through his hands, and so he may have gone directly to the prefect.

As to what Zhang was hoping for, one can only speculate. One Ming poet-farmer, Liu Song, recorded his own thoughts as he worked in his garden, noting how the melon seeds in his hand, when planted, would need plenty of space for their vines to spread; how the melons should already be fruiting since the weeds were flowering so well; and how the fruits should ripen deliciously.[22] But we have no such record of Zhang Guan's thoughts. When did he notice the anomaly? What discussions ensued among kin and neighbors over the course of the growing season as the melons swelled? Zhang's wife had given birth again just the year before; what ambitions for his young sons were expressed? Six or seven early-Ming Jurong men won office by being recommended for their virtue or talent. Perhaps Zhang Guan thought his offering would lead to an official position. Perhaps he hoped to, as the saying is, "Present a melon and receive a jade."[23] Instead, he was sent home with 1,200 cash and an imperial ode, which he must have proudly inscribed on a stone stele, though none survives.[24] Locals had choices about how to understand anomalies, and whether to present them to the throne. After 1372, Jurong men did not send lucky fruits to the emperor. They went back to using melon omens to commend good magistrates instead of the emperor—perhaps because of the tragedy that befell Zhang Guan and his family.

Chapter IV

The Zhang Family

The 1496 Jurong county gazetteer includes Zhang Guan in its section on virtuous or righteous local men (*yishi* 義士). The brief biography mentions that he presented to the emperor some auspicious melons his vegetable garden had produced. Everyone, the biography reports, admired Guan's devotion to his sovereign and to his younger brother, Qian. Some years after the melon incident, Qian was wrongly arrested for a crime committed by someone else of the same name. He was sent to the capital in chains and thrown into prison.

Such a wrongful arrest was hardly unusual at the time (probably about 1390). As Taizu's paranoia grew, he arrested and executed tens of thousands of people on suspicion of conspiring with top ministers and generals to overthrow him, or for various kinds of corruption. He set aside normal judicial procedure, encouraging locals to come directly to him with complaints about one another and about officials, and trying cases himself. In the false accusations used to settle old scores, twentieth-century historians could not help seeing parallels to the madness of the Cultural Revolution period (1966–1976), when Mao Zedong oversaw vicious mass popular attacks on teachers, small businessmen, anyone with foreign connections, anyone learned—anyone whose loyalty to Mao was suspect. Some early Ming writers similarly attributed the flood of false accusations in their time directly to the way Taizu's harsh penal practices destroyed kinship ties, community solidarity, and moral authority.[1]

Zhang Guan submitted a petition to the emperor on his brother's behalf—presumably reminding him of the melons—but the plea was in vain. Qian's name was not cleared; instead, Guan was arrested and imprisoned with his brother. Both were sentenced to death. While Qian bemoaned his unjust fate (*ming* 命, as in *tian ming*, the Mandate of Heaven), Guan made the onlookers weep by declaring: "... if [even] one's neighbor were in trouble, one would help him. How much less could I, as an older brother, have any regrets about dying

37

in an attempt to save my younger brother from difficulties and death?" The onlookers shed tears for them. The Zhang brothers' neighbors and kin considered Guan righteous. They buried the pair together about a mile (3 *li*) south of the Jurong county *yamen*, or magistrate's office, near the South Bridge. They called the tomb the "Righteous Mound" (*Yilong* 義壟).[2]

It is striking that two men beheaded as criminals were given such a monument. It is not clear whether the name was given to the grave right away, but it was certainly called that by about 1450, and probably earlier. If the Zhangs suffered any local disgrace because of the executions, it was gone a century later, when Magistrate Wang, local gentryman Wang Shao, and others compiled the 1496 Jurong county gazetteer. The gazetteer proudly included the family and presented Guan's misfortune in the best possible light. Even before the gazetteer was written, some other people surnamed Zhang, who may have been closely related to Guan and Qian, had been honored. Several Zhangs who like those of Guan's line were identified in the 1496 gazetteer as being from the county seat or nearby (*fang guo* 坊郭) and whose written names shared elements with the names of Guan's descendants in ways suggesting a family relationship were honored in the Chenghua period for longevity or literary attainments, or as low-level degree holders.[3] But it was Zhang Guan's own line that earned the greatest honors and reconciled the family with the dynasty.

Zhang Guan died for his brother without regret, as an exemplar of brotherly affection. The relationship of elder and younger brother was one of the five basic relationships that made up society. In each paired relationship, each partner had responsibilities to the other, and living out these relations according to cultural ideals was understood as a way to cultivate one's own best moral nature. The first relationship was parent-child: the parent ideally loving and guiding, the child filial and obedient. The second was ruler-minister, a relationship ideally based in mutual respect, with benevolence on one side and loyalty on the other, although we have already seen how complex it was in practice. The relations between husband and wife, and friend and friend, were complicated too, as people well knew, and so was brotherhood. Brotherly harmony was highly valued. The *Book of Songs* describes a family feast after a sacrificial ceremony:

Numerous are the rushes by the road . . .
Their leaves are clustering.
Beloved are brothers,
None are absent, all cleaving together.[4]

For as long as possible, brothers would live and eat together with their parents in the parental home, which could be added onto as needed. (Daughters usually, and normatively, left their natal families and even their natal villages when they married.) Property was held jointly by all the male members of the family. It was managed, but not fully owned, by the patriarch. Each member contributed his or her labor and wages to the family pot.

Wives, outsiders to the extended family, were often seen as disrupting brotherly harmony. They alone held private property, in the form of the money, clothes, jewelry, and land they had brought as dowry, and although they might choose to lend or give it to the larger family, legally that property went only to their own biological children. Since this arrangement represented a private interest within the common household, women were thought to distract their husbands from their duties to their parents and brothers, and to prefer their own children to others in the same household. A poem from the Han period describes the bitter life of an orphan boy whose sister-in-law comes between him and his elder brother, with whom he lives. The younger boy works hard harvesting melons and pulling them to market on a cart. One day, the cart tips, and the passersby, instead of helping, heartlessly take and eat the melons. The stalks they return to him as proof of the disaster cannot save him from a scolding.[5]

When the strains between brothers' nuclear families became too much to bear, whether they were the fault of the women who married in or not, the joint family property was divided among them with scrupulous equality, with shares sometimes exchanged to keep resources such as shops intact. The arrangements were always overseen by neighbors and kin, and recorded in written agreements. Division was signified by separate residences or at least separate stoves: the brothers no longer ate together. The few families that could remain undivided for generations were greatly admired as seedbeds of virtue. In earlier dynasties they had been honored by the state, although Taizu's mistrust of local elite families with large land-holdings led him to discontinue this practice.[6] Despite the admiration for such multi-generational clans, and the high value placed on extended families, most people throughout Chinese history lived in nuclear or stem families (parents, one child and spouse, and grandchildren) made up of about five people.

Resources could be protected by kinship organizations beyond the family. Early in history, but particularly with the rising affluence and broader gentry society of the late Ming and Qing periods, many families whose brothers had divided generation after generation, but who retained connections as clans, organized themselves into higher-level social bodies with corporate property, a management structure, and written regulations. These organized lineages compiled extensive family trees, usually tracing all male members back to the first ancestor who had settled in the area. Often they invented claims, more and more grandiose with each new edition of the genealogy, to be descended from a well-known figure in history. This process is at work in Xie Jin's *Veritable Records*, where the account of Taizu's ancestors refers back to high antiquity, at least as far back as 1000 B.C.:

> His ancestors were the descendants of Lord Zhuanxu [of antiquity]. King Wu of Zhou enfeoffed his progeny at Zhu; during the Chunqiu period (722–481 B.C.) his descendants left the county and formed the clan of Zhu. For generations they made their home at the Xiang County of the State of Pei, and sometime later some of them moved to Jurong. For generations they were a great clan, and people called their settlement Zhujiaxiang (Zhu Family Lane). [Taizu's forefathers] accumulated goodness for generations but they remained confined to the fields and villages.[7]

The genealogies in which lineages preserved and extended these family trees also included other documents such as family regulations.

Bound now in a cheap notebook cover sporting a 1971 quote from Chairman Mao and held in the Jurong county archive is an 1877 genealogy of a branch, eleven generations deep, of the Zhang family from Jurong's Ge village (southwest of the county seat). It contains family regulations left by the Zhang founding ancestor, referred to as Taizu. The regulations show both the importance of brotherly harmony in the extended, property-sharing family and the psychological strains of such an arrangement. Referring first to the parent-child relationship, Zhang Taizu exhorts his descendants to be filial sons: to study hard, and to earn glory for their parents. Then comes an essay on brotherhood. Lamenting that there are brothers who fall out, or even become enemies, because of small jealousies or conflicts over petty profit, the essay suggests that although a family might no longer be able to have several hundred people under the same roof, brothers could at least refuse to listen to false stories told by trouble-makers, and talk matters out face to face when questions arise. Nowadays, Zhang Taizu laments, people talk about the relationship between husband and wife (and indeed, in the vibrant urban culture of the late Ming period and into the Qing period great emphasis was placed on marital love), but it is good brotherly relations that are the most important. Zhang Taizu wrote:

> Brothers are those people who have the same *qi* as oneself, but a different form. When young they eat from the same bowl and sleep under the same quilt. From the time when their hair is in [childhood] tufts until the time it turns white may be as many as sixty or seventy years. No closer relation can be found in heaven or earth![8]

Clearly, this is how Zhang Guan felt, as he gave up his life alongside his brother, and he passed his values on to his son, Zhang Yi.

When the brothers Guan and Qian were executed and buried, Guan's elder son Zhang Da was exiled, and Yi, the younger son, voluntarily followed him.[9] Their exile was not beyond the boundaries of the Ming empire, but out to a military colony on the borders of civilization, and far from their comfortable home base in Jurong.

The Zhang men did not leave Jurong alone, nor did the petty jealousies of wives pry them apart. Instead, the Zhang daughters and wives won their own reputations for heroic virtue, enhancing the stability and standing of the Zhang family as a whole. The pattern for the women of the family had been set by Guan and Qian's grandmother, Madame Wang, wife of Zhang Jinfu. Widowed when her son, Wencong, was in swaddling clothes, she raised him in respectability and preserved her chastity until her death at age ninety—that is, for sixty-two years. Madame Wang (gentry wives were referred to by their maiden names) exemplified one path to great honor, based on two of the human relationships: parent-child and husband-wife. Husband and wife, like Heaven and Earth or ruler and minister, were not equals, but complements. A man had only one primary wife at a time. The primary wife was chosen by a young man's parents, was married into the family with great ceremony, and brought with her a dowry. She was her husband's partner, and it was her task to manage all the "inside" affairs of the household—not only the cooking, sewing, cleaning, and so on, not only caring for the husband's parents and offering sacrifices to his ancestors, but also keeping the accounts, educating the children, training and overseeing servants, and even managing lands and businesses. A man's success at study, office-holding, or trade depended on his wife's running his affairs properly; when he was away from home she fulfilled his filial duty to care for his parents, as well as the children whom it was his filial duty to produce or adopt.

To be considered a good wife, a gentry woman did not need to bear children herself.[10] Adoption was common and legal. If a wife were barren, or if in her later years she practiced celibacy as a lay Buddhist, her husband might take a secondary wife. Taking a second wife was common among men who were well off enough to afford it. Secondary wives, referred to as "concubines," were bought in exchange for money, and they came into the family without ceremony or dowry. A concubine's children belonged to the wife. If the wife died, a man could marry again, taking a new wife called a "successor wife," who would assume the former wife's ritual obligations and other duties. A concubine was not supposed to be raised to this status. Further, it was considered a man's right to sleep with the maids of the household, provided that he later either raised them to the status of concubine or married them off at the proper time.

Although men had this latitude, by Ming times, a respectable gentry woman slept with only one man in her lifetime. Many widows remarried in spite of this custom, often finding that they could not afford to live alone, or did not wish to remain single. But increasingly over time, society and the state frowned upon widow remarriage and celebrated widow chastity. To resist all pressures from parents, parents-in-law, and suitors to remarry, to resist the lure of sex and company, to manage financially by oneself and raise one's children alone—this was truly admirable. By the late Ming period, the imperially-granted arches that honored chaste widows lined the streets of some towns. Qing gazetteers included such long lists of chaste widows that often few details were provided, but in the Ming period these women's stories were still told, like that of Madame Wang, Zhang Jinfu's wife.

Madame Zhang, personal name Shouzhen ("Preserve Chastity"), may have been a sister of Jinfu. She too set a high standard. She was married to a young boy, which was not uncommon, especially if the bride's family was in financial difficulties. In such cases, sexual intercourse would be delayed until both partners were of a suitable age, and maybe even longer, depending on the economic and other circumstances of the family. In this case, Shouzhen's husband was only six when he died, and she was fifteen. There would have been nothing at all improper in her remarrying, since she had not slept with him. Her parents wanted her to remarry, but she swore to follow him in death and succeeded in cutting her throat despite her mother-in-law's attempt to intervene. This fierce commitment to a heroic chastity overrode the virtue of obedience to parents. Widow chastity and suicide could exemplify the moral autonomy of the individual within the family system.

The Zhang women of the next generation faced tragedy with the same iron resolve. Madame Ni, Zhang Qian's widow, went with her nephews Da and Yi into exile; she managed even in a military colony to preserve her chastity. With her were her sister-in-law Zhang Quanyi, who had been widowed earlier and returned to her natal family, and her mother-in-law (Quanyi's mother), whom they served together. (The relationship of daughter-in-law to mother-in-law is not found in the list of five relationships. A bride was supposed to treat her parents-in-law as parents, serving them with filial piety. But of course she could not transfer her affections immediately, and the mother-in-law for her part feared losing her son's affection. The relationship was understood to be a difficult one, but it was crucial in people's lives, and it received much attention in literature.) Da soon died, and Yi was transferred to Chishui military guard in the wilds of northwestern Guizhou. Madame Ni and her sister-in-law Quanyi stayed with Yi after Da's death, apparently traveling around with him for several decades. They died at ages seventy-four and eighty-three, respectively. Quanyi's natal family took care of her in death too—her nephew Yi's sons and grandsons worshipped her in the family temple, along with the tablets of their male ancestors and their wives.

Also traveling with Yi were two other women: his brother Da's wife, Madame Tan, and his own wife, Madame Sun. Tan was widowed at age thirty-one. Left with two young sons, Qi and Lin (named after the mythical unicorn, *qilin*), she supported them for years and taught them well while serving her mother-in-law, Madame Hu. Tan died at age sixty-six, after spending thirty-five years as a widow. In her final illness, she turned over the affairs of the household to her junior sister-in-law, Yi's wife, Madame Sun. None of these women remarried: they devoted their lives to caring for their husbands' families. Even Quanyi, who returned to her natal family, did not marry again.

Madame Sun too shows a sense of rectitude that goes far beyond passive acquiescence in patriarchal norms. She earned a long biography in the 1750 edition of the gazetteer, even though her husband lived until he was past eighty. Her chastity had been demonstrated at the beginning, rather than the end, of the marriage. Here is her story: she was the daughter of a close friend of Zhang Guan, so close that the two men adopted the same literary "style" name, a kind of public name men chose for themselves. Both called themselves Gubin ("Grain Guest"). When the friends' wives were expecting, the two Gubins betrothed their unborn children. This was a common way for men or women to express friendship or cement a relationship with maternal kin. (Paternal kin, who shared a surname, were forbidden to marry.) But when the two children were only ten years old, Zhang "Gubin" Guan was executed and the Zhang family went into exile. When later, at his mother's command, Zhang Yi went to Jurong to claim Miss Sun as his bride, her father, Sun "Gubin," understandably wanted to back out of the agreement. Such a marriage would ally him with executed criminals and doom his daughter to a life in exile. His daughter sternly lectured him: "When I was in the womb, you allowed [the betrothal]. To back out of it now because of trouble and misfortune is not right!" She took the moral high ground, but it is also quite possible that she loved Yi, having grown up expecting to marry him. Her father had to give in, and Sun followed Yi into exile. Finding that her mother-in-law had passed away, she served her elder sister-in-law Tan and the various other senior women of the family as if they were her mother-in-law. She proved a worthy partner to Zhang Yi.[11]

The family's redemption from disaster lay in the hands of these women, and in the hands of Zhang Guan's son and grandson: Zhang Yi, first and foremost a family man, and Zhang Jian, a filial son and faithful servant of the Ming state. After Yi's marriage to

Madame Sun, his mother died, and he managed the funeral and "wasted away in mourning" (i.e., properly completed all the funeral and mourning rites). Still a young man of about twenty, eager to learn, Yi traveled from place to place studying with various Confucian teachers. Like Ming Taizu himself and like Zhang Taizu of Ge village, Yi later composed and enforced family instructions that were much admired. He carefully taught his sons and his nephews, and carried on his father Guan's intense brotherly loyalty, loyalty that extended to his father's brothers and that demanded even death for its fulfillment. His epitaph reports: "Once, his uncle Gushan was gravely ill. Mr. Zhang quickly prayed to Heaven, asking to shorten his own life to extend his uncle's. The illness healed. When Zhang Yi himself was close to death he only ordered his various sons to divide the funeral paraphernalia in two [so that one portion could] serve his younger brother [Boqi]."[12] To show concern for his brother's proper burial even before the brother took sick was not morbid, but loving. Children often prepared their parents' burial clothes, and even their coffins, long ahead of time, to reassure them that they would be properly buried. Yi was willing to die for his father's brother, and he thought about his brother's needs on his death bed. Another Jurong man, perhaps a relative, went further: the 1496 gazetteer reports that Zhang Wenli 張文禮 and Zhang Wende 德 were brothers who loved each other and were the same in everything. When Wenli died, Wende stopped eating, and on his deathbed he instructed his twelve sons and nephews to bury him with his brother.[13]

Yi insisted, even on the borders of civilization, on following his parents' instructions not to divide the property, but to keep one household and one stove. So the inner affairs of Yi's household, which Madame Sun took over as Tan's health failed, were complicated. In the household there were at least three women senior to Sun, at least two nephews, and Sun's own sons, Jian, Mengzhao (given name unknown), and possibly others. Jian (1406–1471) had two sons by a wife *née* Wang, and two more by a concubine surnamed He, and four daughters, perhaps by his successor wife surnamed Shen. Yi's younger brother, styled Boqi, was there with his own family, and another brother of the older generation may have had his family there as well. Sun deftly managed the finances of this large extended family, who all lived and ate together, remaining in exile from Jurong from about 1390 to about 1454.

The household economy was managed by the wife of the oldest man even in peasant households, a custom that lasted for centuries. Communist leader Zhu De, describing his childhood in a late nineteenth-century China impoverished by natural disaster, Qing fiscal mismanagement, overpopulation, and the direct and collateral effects of Western imperialism, told American reporter Agnes Smedley:

> My grandmother organized and directed the entire household economy. She allotted each member his or her task, the heavy field work to the men, the lighter field work and household tasks to the women and children. Each of her four daughters-in-law took their turn, a year at a time, as cook for the entire family, with the younger children as helpers. The other women spun, sewed, washed, cleaned or worked in the field. At dawn each morning the daughter-in-law who was cook for that year arose, lit the fire, and started breakfast. When we heard my grandfather moving about, all the rest of us also got up and went immediately about our chores. . . . My grandmother . . . also rationed the food according to age, need, and the work being done.[14]

And at the end of each year Zhu's grandmother and her eldest son shared out the year's income and decided who needed new clothes. Then she put whatever money could be saved into a jar and buried it under her bedroom floor. Zhu's description of how the grandmother managed the entire family stands side by side with his comments that girls were too insignificant to need the ugly nicknames that were given to boys to protect them from the jealousy of evil spirits, and that "a woman's duty was to work and bear sons who could carry on the family line and provide labor power for the family. She had no individual rights whatever."[15] And both kinds of comments were true. Patriarchy was a complex system that oppressed young brides and concubines but gave responsibility and honor to wives of strong character who survived into old age.

By preserving the family as a center of moral rectitude so far from home, Zhang Yi and his wife Madame Sun were also contributing to the state. The connection of individual, family, state, and world appears clearly in a text called the "Great Learning" (*Da xue* 大學). In the Song period, the Neo-Confucian movement had applied the teachings of Confucius to a wider range of people than before, and had developed new cosmological theories, spiritual practices, and institutions to compete with Buddhism. The great twelfth-century Neo-Confucian Zhu Xi had pulled the "Great Learning" out of the classic *Record of Rites* to stand on its own as one of the Four Books. Early in Taizu's rise to power, a scholar presented him with a copy of the "Great Learning," answering his question about governing by saying: "It's all in this book."[16] A basic text for the civil service examinations, the "Great Learning" was memorized by every literate person and was known to and taken seriously by many illiterate people as well.

It begins by explaining that to act morally and effectively one must first understand for oneself what is fundamental.

> The Way of the Great Learning lies in manifesting bright virtue, in being close to the people, and in resting in the highest good. By knowing where to stop, one can achieve stability. When there is stability, there is peace; when there is peace, then one can think things through, and when one can think things through, one will "get it." Things have their roots and branches; matters have their results and causes. If one knows what is primary and what comes after, then one can draw near the Way.

The text then explains how the individual—originally understood as only the ruler, but by Ming times as any individual, or at least any educated male—could contribute to the world by cultivating his or her own moral nature. The utopian society of the "Great Learning" is woven together from top to bottom in one moral quest and is said to have been realized in the distant past.

> The ancients who wished to illuminate bright virtue in the whole world first governed their own countries. Wishing to govern their countries, they first regulated their families. Wishing to regulate their families, they first cultivated their own moral character. To cultivate their moral character, they first straightened their heart/minds. To straighten their heart/minds, they first made sure their intentions were sincere. To make their intentions sincere, they first extended their knowledge, and to extend their knowledge, they investigated things.

Zhang Yi studied ("investigated things") and "extended his knowledge" by learning from various Confucian teachers. He made his intentions sincere and straightened out his heart, so that even in moments of crisis he immediately knew the right thing to do: offer his life to save his uncle and plan for his brother's burial when he himself was sick. He and Sun regulated their large family, teaching and managing the group—including its financial affairs—so well that their son Jian earned a *jinshi* degree, the highest degree in the civil service examinations, and contributed directly to governing the country. Although Yi himself never held office, he came from a gentry family that well understood standards of behavior and textual learning, and that smoothed the operation of the world by their actions and inner rectitude.

The facts about Yi's life come from an epitaph written by Ni Qian, who earned his *jinshi* degree in 1439, the same year as Jian. "Graduating" together often served as the basis for a personal relationship, but in this case the Ni family was from nearby Shangyuan county and may have married into the Zhang family as well. (Ni Qian's son Yue also wrote an epitaph for Jian when he died.) Of course an epitaph such as Ni's was laudatory. It would have been based on Ni's personal knowledge of his friend Jian's father, as well as on stories the family told him or gave him in writing. Epitaphs have sometimes been denigrated as sources because of their positive slant, and because they fit men into pre-existing stereotypes: the good official, the filial son, the learned recluse, the wild poet. Yet epitaphs are not all the same. Explaining the views of an eighteenth-century scholar, David Nivison points out that each level of history—history of family (genealogy), locality (gazetteer), reign period (*Veritable Records*), and dynasty (official history)—builds on the details of the lower ones. He continues:

> It is a commonplace to say of old China that there the family was everything, the individual nothing. This calls attention to something true, but as a total judgement it is surely misleading. After all, in Chang's view of historical writing, the life and work of an individual man formed the basis of everything else. And how many of us, I wonder, have ever thought of writing a biographical sketch of a dead relative or friend? Yet it was taken for granted . . . in eighteenth-century China that this final act of respect for the value of an individual human life was only a gentleman's duty.[17]

In writing the epitaph, Ni Qian stressed three aspects of Zhang Yi's life story. Preservation of the family as a center of moral rectitude and Jian's success as an official were two; the third was Yi's return home. Even after a generation in exile, the Zhangs were strongly connected to Jurong. Like Wang Shao, who gave up office-holding and returned to Jurong for the good life of poetry and wine, Yi took his style name from his return home. An epitaph for Yi's son Jian reports that even in exile Yi "studied books and respected the rites, and the border barbarians respected and trusted him. Late [in life] he returned to his native village. People called him the Elder of Jurong."[18] Ni Qian's funerary verse for Yi says: "Even among barbarians, he practiced loyalty, good faith, sincerity, and respect. When old he returned, not forgetting his beginnings [but] delighting in his place of birth." "In his last years," Ni writes, "he thought of his old place. Taking along his family, he returned east."[19] The 1750 gazetteer is more explicit: Yi "thought of the old garden and mound," where the melons had grown and where his father and uncle were buried.[20] When Yi arrived in Jurong, he was youthful and gay. His neighbors marveled that although in his eighties he looked as lively as Lao Laizi, a fabled and filial graybeard who acted like a child to entertain his parents and make them feel young. But as if returning from ignominious exile with a large family and a successful son at his side had fulfilled the purpose of his life, Zhang Yi fell ill and died soon afterward, in about 1456.[21]

Yi's son Jian completely reversed the family disgrace. His life united border, court, and locality, and brought together family and dynasty in a web of travail. Jian, after studying with his father, followed his brother Mengzhao to seek a teacher in Lüzhou, but when Jian arrived, Mengzhao died. Jian attended to his brother's burial and then returned home. His next teacher also died, leaving Jian to manage his posthumous affairs. Finally, under the wing of yet another teacher, Jian earned his *jinshi* degree in 1439, and with it a ceremonial arch in his home town.[22] Jian advanced steadily through the eighteen ranks of the bureaucracy, from messenger (rank 8a) to investigating censor (7a) to governor of the northern capital prefecture Shuntian (3a). Whether because he submitted a memorial to the emperor asking that military expenditures be reduced to lessen the people's difficulties (one biography characterizes the criticism in the memorial as "straight talk"), or because he and another official impeached each other, as was not an infrequent occurrence in the factional battles of the bureaucracy, he was demoted to prefect of Laizhou in Shandong (4a). According to his death notice in the *Veritable Records*, he made his mark in Laizhou as a good resident administrator, but the local gazetteer records nothing more about him than his name and tenure. After two years he was recalled to the capital to be chief minister of the court of the imperial stud (3b).

His early training in military matters apparently served him well, for he personally trained militiamen to fight the coastal bandits who were plaguing the southeastern province of Fujian when he was posted there to oversee taxation. Jian served for twenty-two years, up to the very day of his death in 1471. His death notice in the *Veritable Records* praises his diligence in office, his attention to detail in serving the people, and his sincere filiality.[23]

Zhang Jian left office only twice, both times for his parents. According to the seamless idea of moral cultivation and effective ruling presented in the "Great Learning" and other works, filial piety and loyal service were connected. Ming Taizu himself had explained the connection to a group of new officials.

> As soon as you left your mother's body and were seen to be a boy, your mother told your father, who was overjoyed when he heard it. At two months your parents watched you sleep and laugh, and were pleased. At a year you recognized your parents and so moved them to happiness. Then you crawled or crept or held onto something and stood up, and your parents then became very happy. . . . Your parents worried about your getting near fire or water for fear you might burn or drown yourself in your ignorance. They were careful to keep cold from you in winter and the bugs away from you in summer. Your parents' burdens were beyond telling.[24]

Filiality had its roots in the earliest moments of human life, but as John Dardess explains, in Taizu's thinking it encompassed all ethical behavior. It meant not only visiting one's parents first thing in the morning and last thing at night, serving them food and drink, and obeying them, but also *resisting* their orders if they contravened ritual or law, maintaining the family financially, avoiding any misconduct that might invite reproof and any criminal action that would bring punishment, serving in office with seriousness or on the battlefield with bravery, choosing upright friends, and acting properly in human relationships. Taizu lamented that few men indeed, even those selected for honors because of their filial piety, really understood it.[25]

For many people, mourning was perhaps the most important moment in the filial relation, and here too the connection between state service and filiality is shown. As a Portuguese observer wrote: "The mourning which they use is the sharpest that ever I saw, for they wear gowns after the common sort of very coarse wool next to the flesh, and girt with great cords."[26] Sons in government office, no less than sons in other professions, were expected to mourn their parents' deaths for three years (usually understood as two years plus three months). Leaving office to care for a sick or aging parent was also possible, and it was a useful way to retire from sticky situations. For example, when the young Xie Jin, later Yongle's propagandist, went one step too far in provoking Ming Taizu in 1391, the emperor ordered him to devote himself to the care of his aged father at home for ten years, as a way of forcing him to leave the court. But leaving public life to mourn a parent's death was not optional. It was expected in bureaucratic procedure and absolutely required by Ming public opinion. Xie Jin, hearing of Taizu's death in 1398, was so desperate to return to court to pay homage to the ruler who had explicitly ordered him to stay home that he left in the middle of the period of mourning for his mother, thus incurring further displeasure from the administration.[27] A prominent late Ming grand secretary, the right-hand man of the young Wanli emperor and his mother, caused a furor among officials nationwide when he agreed to the empress dowager's request that he remain in the capital instead of returning home to mourn his father.[28] The Qing emperors gradually reversed this expectation by requiring important officials to "mourn at their posts," which opened a conceptual gap between duty to parents and to sovereign that had long been papered over.[29]

In Zhang Jian's case, there was no gap. He left office first to mourn his mother, showing heroic filial piety by living for three years in a hut at her grave. His grief and sincerity called forth an auspicious response: a strange flock of birds gathered in the trees. The second interruption in his career came after his success in office had earned honorary titles for his parents and wives. He accompanied his father home to Jurong, and when Yi fell ill the following year, Jian waited on him day and night with soup and medicine, never leaving his side. When Yi died, Jian again spent three years at the grave. This time, miraculous fungus grew beside the mound. According to one report, Jian became known as Mr. Filial Fungus Zhang (*Xiao Zhi Zhang Shi* 孝芝張氏).[30] The testaments to Jian's filiality congratulate both him and his parents, who raised him so well under adverse circumstances. One could argue that the signs also implicitly congratulate the emperor who secured the services of such a paragon. Jian's promotion from messenger to censor immediately after the mourning for his mother may have come partly in recognition of his filiality.

Different compilers have construed differently the double meaning of Jian's life; some emphasize his service to the state, some to the family. Wan Sitong's draft of the history of the whole Ming dynasty appends Jian's biography to that of another, unrelated, Zhang, a Shandong man who earned imperial commendation in the Yongle period because several hundred young crows cried mournfully in the trees for three years, twice, as he resided by his parents' tomb. For Wan, the meaning of Zhang Jian's life too lay in his being so filial that his mourning hut "caused a sympathetic response from a flock of birds and fungus plants."[31] In the Jurong county gazetteer, however, the reader first encounters the Zhang family in the shape of the ceremonial arch erected to celebrate Jian's *jinshi* degree. For the gazetteer compilers, the miraculous resonances of Jian's filial devotion and his service to the state were equally important. And they were connected. As the funerary verse by Shang Lu for Zhang Jian says:

> Mr. Zhang's forebears
> for generations were sincere in filiality and friendship.
> The roots were stable,
> so the leaves and branches were both luxuriant:
> thus they produced a chief minister.[32]

A healthy family produced filiality and loyalty together. The honor of the filial son reflected well on the state he served, and the honor of the hardworking official reflected well on the native place that claimed him.

Shang Lu's verse, and the "Great Learning," move directly from family to state, but often there was an intermediate focus of loyalty: the native place. Localities specialized in certain natural and cultural products, which were sent in to the capital as tribute and were also sold all over the empire: Huzhou's writing brushes, used for both painting and calligraphy, were famous; Jinhua is still known for its salty ham. People took pride in local products. For example, the painter Xu Wei 徐渭 (1521–1593), was from northern Zhejiang province, which like Jurong was in the cultural heartland known as "Jiangnan," and he championed a local style of painting. Using a kind of paper that gazetteers list as a special product of his home prefecture, he frequently painted images of fish, crabs, melons, and vegetables, and he always wrote on such paintings the following verse:

> The fragrance of fish and crabs, melon and bamboo shoots,
>   vegetables and legumes;
> One section of "stream-vine" paper, small and square.
> If you compare them to other things, they are all winter flavors.
> Only Jiangnan has these local specialties.[33]

Men from the same county also sought one another out when far from home and, in the Qing period in particular, formed organized guilds to deploy native-place ties in business and government. The reality of local ties was the rationale behind the law of avoidance, whereby a man could not hold government office in or near his home town. Yet like all other ties, the tie of locality was complex. On the one hand, as the plague of false accusations during Taizu's reign suggests, neighbors could be deadly enemies as well as allies. Social competition from the home town could carry over into the national arena. And, on the other hand, it was not always clear what a man's "home town" was. Zhang Jian, for example, was claimed by two native places.

Jian and his father, Yi, lived most of their lives in exile from Jurong. Jian was neither born nor brought up there. Guizhou, their place of exile, was eager to claim them. The 1555 gazetteer for Guizhou province lists both Yi and Jian as men of the Chishui military colony.[34] Qing poetry collector and Guizhou native Chen Tian proudly labels Zhang Jian a native of Chishui and points out: "Our Guizhou's having *jinshi* degree holders began with Mengbi [i.e., Jian]."[35] Chen probably drew his information on Jian from a Ming compilation of biographies that reports Jian's unusually smooth career and the responses of fungus and birds to his filial mourning. In fact, that compilation, which categorizes Ming men by province and prefecture, lists Jian twice, apparently without realizing it: once as a Chishui man, once as a Jurong man. Some of the facts given are the same, such as the story of Jian's mourning for his parents; both mention the fungus that grew in response. But the Guizhou version is much more detailed, probably because it was unusual for a Guizhou man to have so successful a career.[36]

Jian's one surviving poem, anthologized by Chen Tian, suggests that he did identify with Guizhou, where he was born and raised.

"Looking to Antiquity"
The heart we are given transmits the [knowledge of the] flourishing
    [age of antiquity];
Study of the classics again opens the [way of] governance.
The study of the classics prospers in both Ba and Peng
    [in Sichuan, also outside the cultural heartland];
their fame and virtue have become our model.
[Guizhou's] Zangke region is wild indeed,
hemmed in by these towering peaks.
How can one start up prefectures and counties?—
The worthies and heroes have already broken the trail!
Human civilization has extended to all of China,
between heaven and earth encompassing all differences.
Therefore I know that intelligent and heroic scholars
cannot be held back by [their native environment of] hills and streams.
Now it has been a long time, several generations.
How long-lasting their impact on us!
Looking to antiquity—a long sigh.
Bearing a heavy anxiety, I have been cut off at the knees.[37]

Jian's poem expresses a sense of himself as a man of a backward place, where civilization does reach, but where it is difficult to really accomplish anything. In fact, he might have been able to reinvent himself as a Guizhou man to leave the family disgrace behind. Because of the exile, the Zhang family was registered as a military family. Had Jian further registered for the examinations as a Guizhou native, passing might have been easier, since there was a geographical quota system. Yet he did not do so.[38] Instead, as we shall see, he kept the family history alive, and it was included in his biographies, which often begin with a short account of the melon audience, and sometimes of the unhappy aftermath.[39] Jurong reciprocated Jian's loyalty. Both Yi and Jian were celebrated in the Jurong gazetteers; both were worshipped in an official temple in Jurong as local worthies.[40] And both were buried alongside the executed brothers Guan and Qian, Yi's father and uncle, south of town, at the "Righteous Mound."[41]

The tomb's name and location south of the county seat resonated with a monument to another local man also honored in the temple to local worthies: a Tang-period filial son named Zhang Changwei 張常洧. Like Jian centuries later, but even more single-mindedly, Changwei showed his filiality by taking mourning to an extreme. He resided by his parents' grave in mourning for more than thirty years. During that time, a thousand strange trees grew up, a flock of white crows came flying, and twelve miraculous fungi appeared, like those that had congratulated Jian. The *fengshui*, the natural forces of *qi* that could be channeled through graves or buildings to assist humans, at this parental grave was very good—so good that in the Song period the government moved the grave to build the county school there.[42] (It was here that the stele recording Song Magistrate Zhang Kan's auspicious melons was preserved.) In the Qing period, the Confucian temple at the school complex still had a porch named for the thousand cypress trees that had once stood there, and a lone survivor was still called "the tomb tree." Although the parents of this local paragon were displaced by a state institution, the sense that the grave's original location was their place lingered.

When the filial Zhang Changwei himself died, he was honored in 789 with a construction called the Yitai 義臺 (Righteous Platform). It was directly south of the county seat in front of his parents' tomb that became the county school.[43] In Ming times, Changwei was claimed by a clan of Zhangs in Jurong from a village east of the county seat. These Zhangs must have had considerable status in the early Ming period, for none other than Taizu's adviser, Song Lian himself, in early 1372, penned a preface to their genealogy. They studied hard, working out a system whereby they had one man specializing in each of the classics for the civil service examinations. They were so prominent locally that, as Song wrote, if you asked who the locally respected families were, the answer would be, "Well, first, there are the Daiting Zhang; and then, there are the Daiting Zhang."

Being named "Zhang" is like being named "Smith" or "Martinez." Was Zhang Guan related to these prominent Zhangs? As with the question of Jian's native place, there is not a completely straightforward answer. The construction of a lineage identity and organization was slow and complicated. Song Lian's preface and others stress that records had been lost; an earlier, 1343 preface laments that of ten thousand million sections of genealogies only one or two were saved from destruction in the ravages of war. Yet that lack of documentation did not prevent the Ming-era Daiting Zhang from laying claim to a Song official with the same name as Zhang Guan's brother, Qian 謙, and to the more distant and more dramatic Tang filial son Changwei. By the middle of the Ming period, the Daiting Zhang had populated seventeen other villages and were identified—first in 1455 in a preface by Wu Jie, whom we will meet again in Chapter 7—as the Jurong or Juqu Zhang clan (Juqu being a poetic name for Jurong that refers to the hook shape of Mount Mao). But then in about 1530, Magistrate Wang Shen 王紳 accidentally discovered Zhang Changwei's long-abandoned monument, the Yitai. He identified it by consulting old gazetteers, and renovated it to teach local people about filial piety by shaming those who did not mourn properly when their parents had died. Only after that, in 1536, did a Zhang claiming to be a relative have an old inscription for Changwei properly recarved. In 1562, a stele with five characters etched in outline, reading "Filial Son Zhang's Righteous Platform" (*Zhang Xiaozi Yitai* 張孝子義臺) was set up. (By 1900 the left corner was missing, but the stele had been embedded in the back wall of the shrine.)[44] It was at about this time that an ancestral temple was built on the old site of the Yitai and that the clan, scattered throughout the county, began using the name "Yitai Zhang" and holding joint feasts at the Yitai.[45] In the Wanli period, an old Jin-period (c. 400) tile reading "Zhang Zhuangwu ci" 張壯武祠 was found. According to Jin historical sources, this Zhang was a nobleman who had escaped trouble by crossing the river southward and had made his home in Jurong. The tile was embedded in the wall of the Righteous Platform, at a time when clan members were repairing it. There was no evidence that the nobleman Zhang had any connection with the Yitai Zhang, but they claimed him by a process of bricolage that was typical of the whole lineage-creating process.[46]

Similarly, whether or not Zhang Guan and his family were actually related to the Daiting (later the Yitai) Zhangs, they were surely associated with them. Guan's tomb was located near, perhaps only a third of a mile from, the Yitai. The name "Righteous Mound" (*yilong*) echoes that of the earlier monument. When Song Lian heard that the melons were presented by a Zhang from Jurong, did he think of this clan he had commemorated a few months earlier? Liu Ji, Taizu's other adviser, had spent time in Jurong county; did he know about the Zhangs? And had Zhu Yuanzhang, long before he became emperor Taizu, grown up hearing tales from his Jurong grandparents of these illustrious, studious Zhangs? When he received Mr. Zhang's melons, and wrote an ode wishing him well, did he think back to those tales? If we look further into local history, other facts, and other historical claims, come to light that hint at why Zhang Guan's overture to the Ming ruler went so dramatically wrong.

Chapter V

The Smile of the God

A Jurong Man

Zhu Yuanzhang, Ming Taizu, though he considered himself a Fengyang man, also had roots in Jurong county. Tao Kai and the other ministers were not inventing that fact as they touted the significance of the melons having grown in Jurong. Many sources record that Taizu's ancestors had lived about 20 *li* (6 or 7 miles) west of the county seat, in Zhu Family village, in what is now known as Stone Lion District, named for two ancient tomb guardians that stand in a field.[1] The farmers who grow rapeseed and bury their dead on the slight rise between East and West Dai village will tell the visitor today that it was the site of Taizu's ancestral village—when ploughing, they still turn up tiles and bricks. The Zhu family graves had been there too. The county gazetteers record local traces, oddly retroactive "memories," of the connection with imperial Ming. The 1496 gazetteer lists, in its section on hills and valleys:

> Sleeping Dragon Ridge: About 10 *li* west of the county seat. Zhu Family Village. On top of the ridge stands a tree that has five branches, like the claw of an [imperial] dragon. People call it the 'dragon-claw tree.'[2]

The later edition of the gazetteer (1750), which incorporated much of the earlier one, expanded its treatment of many topics, and added in events that had occurred in the interim, explained that "sleeping dragon ridge" was the location of the old Zhu family cemetery. The local people also called it the "imperial tombs," and they did not dare to gather fuel or graze their animals there, even though there was no prohibition.[3] In fact, there were no longer any Zhu graves there. Early in his reign, Taizu had moved them.

A mid-twentieth century collection of folk stories includes a story about Taizu searching for the old family graves with some sycophantic high officials in tow. Seeing a big tomb in a good place, "he ordered his followers to put some sacrificial offerings in front of the grave. Who could know, that when he made his first obeisance, a crack would open in the grave; at his second obeisance, the crack widened; at his third, the grave sank three feet." It turned out that his family's graves were off to the side, on a small hill, and they were not clearly marked. "Zhu Yuanzhang had no choice but to order his followers to leave some offerings at the foot of the small hill, recognize the hill as his father, and make three kowtows there. Right away, the hill got three feet taller."[4] This story—collected, if not invented, after the fall of the whole imperial system in China—takes kinship seriously but laughs at the pretensions of a social upstart emperor.

In using the names "dragon-claw tree" and "imperial tombs" in "remembering" the Zhu family as imperial and as awesome enough to keep animals off their erstwhile burial ground, Jurong people were transplanting the fruit of later events back into the local seedbed. For when Taizu's family had lived in Jurong, their circumstances had been precarious. His grandfather, one of four brothers, had fled in desperation.[5] As Taizu's writers explained in his voice in a stele erected in the village in Fengyang where he had been born, "In the Yuan [period Our grandfather] was registered as a 'gold-panning' household, and since [metal was] not a local product, he had to conduct trade in other places to meet the annual tax collection. Exhausted by corvée service, Our grandfather the Chuyi Venerable abandoned the fields and house and moved with his two sons."[6]

Perhaps that poverty and flight from tax obligations explain why Taizu downplayed the Jurong connection. Recall that in the conversation about the melons, Tao Kai had to remind him that Jurong was his ancestral home. Zhu had done his best to forget it and construct a new past for himself. Having located the old family graves, he moved them to Fengyang, where he had been born, and where in 1372 he was trying to build a new capital. When the area in Fengyang for the new imperial graveyard had been measured out, some officials proposed moving out the existing graves of commoners to make room. Taizu responded sentimentally: "These are the graves of my family's old neighbors; they should not be moved out." The locals were allowed to come and go on the site to sweep graves at the proper times in spring and autumn.[7] Taizu's loyalty clearly lay with Fengyang. He had little to gain from remembering his family roots in Jurong—not, I would argue, because he had completely transcended them, but precisely because he could not quite do so. Early in his reign, Taizu was still building up his legitimacy, and in Jurong society, a Zhu was no match for a Zhang.[8]

Like Zhang Jian, Taizu was born into a Jurong family, but far from Jurong. Unlike Zhang Jian, he was reluctant to acknowledge the connection, although he did set up a stele there recounting his genealogy. Why should we believe that Jurong was important in the way he understood himself in the world? Why should we think that his parents and grandparents, as well as filling his ears with stories of magic and adventure, had told him stories of the old home place, of their hardships and humiliations there, and of the great families who dominated Jurong society?[9] Perhaps we can make an indirect argument. Each part of China favors a different style of grave, and graves stand in the fields or along the roads, not segregated in cemeteries. In Jinhua, Song Lian's native place, graves are almost pyramidal, with sloped sides and a flat front where the stele is mounted. In Wenzhou, further south in Zhejiang province, the so-called "armchair graves" have curved walls coming out in front on both sides, leading back to the stone stele. In Jurong, graves are round mounds, almost cylindrical at the base, often with a pot on top, and girdled round halfway up their height with (nowadays) concrete walls.

Taizu and his wife, Empress Ma, are buried in the hills of Nanjing, in a vast and beautiful complex called the Xiaoling (Filial Tomb). It took three decades to complete, and it combined old elements with innovations that were then copied for the rest of the imperial period. The complex stretches over a mile and a half, forming the shape of the Big Dipper, as some imperial graves had done for a thousand years.[10] Beginning at an archway where all officials had to dismount, one walks along an invitingly curved spirit way lined with pairs of large stone animals: crouching and standing lions, legendary *xiezhi* beasts, camels (new, and signifying Taizu's pride in having pacified the Western regions of which Song Lian spoke), elephants, *qilin* unicorns, and horses. Now the stones are grey with time, but where visitors have rubbed them the veined stone shows clearly: white with pink for the horses, gray and purple for the camels, the lions of beige with orange, peach, and red veins. The animals are not too large to be forbidding; one can touch noses with some of them. And the path is carefully curved, so that at any time the visitor sees one pair just ahead, the next pair, and one of the following pair. The curve assures a good flow of *qi*; and the result is a comfortable feeling of both connection and awe, very different from the feeling produced by, for instance, fascist architecture designed to diminish the individual.

After passing the animals one passes large figures of civil and military officials and then crosses curved bridges into an aisle of cypress inhabited by strange whistling birds. A few ceremonial buildings, with red walls and yellow glazed-tile roofs, interrupt and hedge the long walk. The buildings are raised on platforms with white stone railings. Gargoyles thrust out their long heads for drain pipes. The first, small building houses a stele erected in Taizu's praise by the Qing emperor Kangxi, and the last is a vast rectangular fort. The ramps of the fort, made in about 1383, are paved in glazed green and yellow tiles, set sideways in strips alternating with cobblestones. Behind the fort is the grave itself, a hill called the "Treasure Mound." Here, the signs and the books tell us, Taizu innovated in the design. Earlier imperial tombs had been square, but he chose a natural hill, about 1,200 feet across and 210 feet high, and rounded it off. The whole mound is surrounded by a wall.[11] Perhaps this innovation simply came from a Jurong man's sense of how graves ought to be shaped for spirits to be comfortably housed. Perhaps the emperor from Jurong is still there: in 1644, when the Manchus conquered China, the sound of crying was heard in the night at the tomb.[12]

The Zhang God

However embarrassed about their Jurong roots, Taizu and his descendants happily acknowledged a connection with a neighboring county, one the founder had merely visited. When Zhu Yuanzhang was "spreading his dragon wings," on military campaign near Lake Tai, he climbed Lidou mountain in Guangde county, south of Jurong, to spy out the land. On the summit he lifted his voice in song, praising the wonderful scene spread out before him. When he came down, he stopped to worship a deity enshrined there, known as Cishan 祠山. The future Taizu asked for a sign from the deity, and received one. One source says he divined in the standard way, by receiving a number that matched a bamboo slip with a fortune

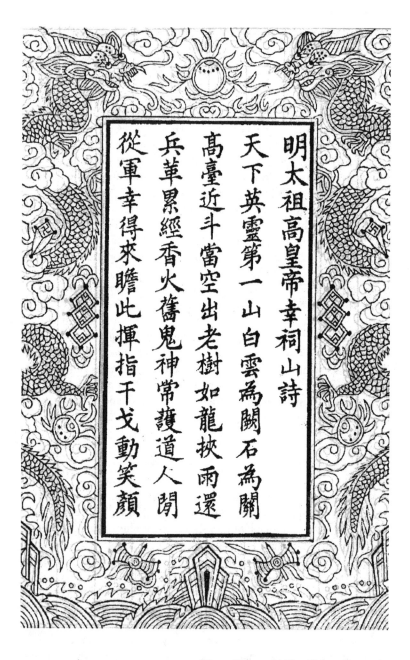

明太祖高皇帝幸祠山詩

天下英靈第一山白雲為闕石為關

高臺近斗當空出老樹如龍挾雨還

兵革累經香火舊鬼神常護道人閒

從軍幸得來瞻此揮指干戈動笑顏

MING TAIZU'S POEM PRAISING CISHAN. From *Cishan zhi* (the *Cishan Gazetter*).

written on it, and that the number he drew was one, the very first slip, presumably a favorable one.[13] Another source says that the idol smiled at him. Taizu left a poem to be inscribed in stone that included the lines:

The central plain is disturbed; when will it be settled?
The brandishing of shields and spears moves the smiling countenance.[14]

The *Cishan Gazetteer* records yet another version of Taizu's encounter with the Cishan deity. The incident occurred in 1356. Taizu's forces were encamped at the base of the mountain, and at night he dreamed that the god showed him a sign that the whole world would be at peace. (Dreams were a common way for deities to communicate with humans.) Because of the dream, he divined the next day at the shrine, and got the same result. This source also gives a longer version of the poem by Ming Taizu, proudly reprinting it on a page bordered with dragons and auspicious signs.

For bravery and numinous power [this is] the number one mountain
    under heaven;
its white clouds make a watchtower, its stones a gate.
High platform nearing the Dipper extends into air;
old trees like dragons bring down rain.
Soldiers, revolts, on and on; the incense fires are old.
Ghosts and gods always protect the leisure of men of the Way.
With the army, I fortunately got to come and gaze upon this.
The brandishing of shields and spears moves the smiling countenance.[15]

Whatever the details of the encounter, Taizu was grateful for the god's encouragement. When he had taken the throne, he first regularly sent court officials to sacrifice to the god in Guangde. In 1388, when this had proved a burden to the local people, Taizu divided the cult in two. Worship in Guangde itself was left in the hands of locals and the subprefect; worship by the court took place in a new temple to Cishan at Jiming mountain just outside the capital, the location of nine other major temples under the Court of Imperial Sacrifices, and of the Directorate of Education, where qualified students were educated for office.[16] The temple was called Cishan Guanghui temple, and national gazetteers describe it as being used "to worship King Zhang Bo 張渤 of Guangde."[17] This Guangde deity was so important that his temple complex had its own 638-page gazetteer, referred to above, which recorded his lineage, his life, the miracles he wrought and the titles he earned, the many buildings of the complex and when they were rebuilt by whom, and all the numerous deities associated with him.[18]

Cishan had granted the arriviste Zhu Yuanzhang honor out of his own large stock. In return, the victorious Taizu had both recognized and honored the deity in his own locality and domesticated his cult into the central roster of sacrifices. Central and local worship were connected, but not unified or identical. Song Na, the high official who memorialized about establishing the temple on Jiming, pointed explicitly to the double nature of worship in the capital and localities in his inscription for the temple, relating it to other doubles like yin and yang, wind and cloud, and being at home or abroad.[19] Worship continued separately at both levels.

Who was this god, Great Emperor Cishan? He was sometimes called Perfected Lord Zhang, but his name in his lifetime during the Han period, most sources agreed, had been Zhang Bo. In the Ming period, Cishan was officially known as "Merciful Great Emperor of the Shrine Mountain (Cishan) Numinousness." Gazetteers disagree about exactly where the deity was born—perhaps in Huzhou—but agree that he manifested his divinity in Guangde. Guangde boasted temples to him dating back to the Tang period or earlier, and the cult flourished there throughout the Ming period. Various stories circulated. One said that his mother had been a female immortal. Another said that he had taken on the form of a huge pig in order to lead demon soldiers in the work of channeling a river and had fled west when his wife improperly caught sight of him in that form. In Qing-period Guizhou, it was believed that he had married his three daughters to Wind, Snow, and Rain. Such tales, and accounts of the god's power to heal and bring rain, sprang from and reinforced local cults to the god that thrived over more than a thousand years. Late Song-period notes record that people at all social levels participated in the cult and its festival. Yixing county, north of Jurong, in the Ming period had ten temples to "Great Emperor Cishan," called "Guanghui branch shrines." The term "branch" meant that they were considered subsidiary to the imperially established temple at Jiming mountain in the capital. Even Cishan's wife had her own temple, with an associated temple fair.[20] The spread of the cult of Cishan, or King Zhang, illustrates a common pattern in popular religion.

The process began when a small shrine was put up to honor an unusual person who had died, or a spirit who had helped someone or had threateningly demanded worship, often in a dream. Local gods actively demanded respect. For instance, the tale is told that a man named Luo once cleared a new field outside his village, intending to raise melons. He set up an altar to the gods and cultivated the young melon plants every morning. But one morning he found a new plaque on the altar, inscribed with black characters. It said: "This is a place set aside for the pleasure of the gods. You may not stay here. Remove your plantings at once." Luo knelt in front of the altar and apologized: "I stupidly thought it permissible for us villagers to propagate crops on this land. If by chance someone is forging this divine directive, let [him] be speedily condemned. If, on the other hand, this is an authentic divine directive, I humbly ask that you change the letters to red as a sign." The next morning, the black letters were red, the color used by the emperor in responding to memorials. Luo apologized again and left the place, abandoning his crop.[21]

In other cases, such local spirits earned attention by answering prayers for help—for sons, health, rain, or the like. When a spirit proved powerful, grateful people made offerings to an image they might gild or clothe. That added to the spirit's power, and as he or she again answered prayers the worshippers would enlarge the shrine, drawing more people. Devotees who traveled as merchants or as migrants might spread the word, setting up shrines elsewhere. Again, as the cult proved efficacious in answering prayers new devotees would make donations to enlarge the shrines, in turn attracting new followers, so that the god could answer more prayers and generate more tales of his or her power. Cults could also fail, of course: in Jurong, a temple was set up to worship a magistrate of the Jin dynasty (317–419) who had benefited the people, but Song Magistrate Zhang Kan converted it into a vinegar factory.[23] But if a cult survived and spread, its devotees would often petition for it to be recognized by the state with a name placard, official patronage, and perhaps a donation.[23]

In the case of Cishan/King Zhang, popular honor had been matched, long before the Ming dynasty, by state recognition. The founder of the Liang dynasty (502–556) centered on Nanjing, moved by a dream, had ended a drought by praying to Cishan for rain and had thanked him with a jade tally of rank.[24] From then on, due to his extraordinary merit in bringing rain, successive dynasties had honored him with official sacrifices and ever-fancier titles. The temple Taizu built for him at Jiming mountain continued this tradition, and Taizu's descendants followed the emperor in worshipping him. In the 1440s, Emperor Zhu Qizhen waffled on whether the throne would fund expensive repairs to the Cishan temple at Nanjing, but in 1461, he approved a censor's request to rebuild the temple to Cishan in Guangde subprefecture. A Qing scholar noted that Cishan's was the only one of the ten early Ming Jiming temples not abandoned. The mutual patronage of the cult and the Ming imperial house continued to be expressed in material exchanges: one of the seven treasures of the temple was presented to the court and then returned.[25]

As mentioned above, the native place of the god was disputed. In 1388, the Cishan temple built at Jiming mountain clearly identified the god as King Zhang Bo of Guangde. But the following year, officials of the Rites Ministry requested imperial permission to set up a stele for the god in Jurong.[26] For Jurong also claimed Cishan. The 1496 Jurong county gazetteer grumped that because there were manifest traces of the god's works in Guangde (perhaps the smile?), the Jurong temple had been demoted to a "branch shrine." There were several shrines to the god in Jurong, but the main temple, referred to by the 1496 gazetteer, stood among several hundred *mou* of Zhang graves south of the county seat. It had a stone pillar behind it, and an artificial pond before it. The temple to "King Zhang" (*Zhang Wang miao* 張王廟) had received the surrounding land as a grant from the throne in the mid-twelfth century. The land grant was associated with Zhang family funerals, but seems to have been made because of the efficacy of the god in responding to prayers for rain. Whenever he was asked, the god would bring the blessing of rain, not only to the immediate area, but to the whole district, which was therefore given the name Fortunate Blessing District (*Fuzuo xiang* 福祚鄉).[27] The 1750 edition of the gazetteer adds:

> Every time it rains for three hours, clouds will rise above the grave. Even until today it has not failed. [The area] behind the temple belongs to the god's descendants. Even until today they have multiplied and flourished. It is also commonly said that the "emperor" is in charge of Jurong's agriculture and irrigation. The villages all have temples to worship him. It is not just this one place.[28]

This evidence shows that the Jurong deity Zhang was clearly identified with the wider cult of Cishan. His main temple stood among the Zhang graves south of the city. There, some time in the twentieth century, the Zhangmiao factory replaced a large and thriving temple to King Zhang, a temple where, according to an aged informant in 2004, people had gone to ask Old Man Zhang (*Zhang Laoye*) for help with family conflicts. Qingming, the day on which family graves are swept and cleaned, was his big festival—as befits a family god.

For King Zhang/Cishan was indeed a family god. The connections are not easy to piece together. Song Na commented in the 1388 inscription for the temple on Jiming mountain that the various statements about Cishan's time and native place "were not without contradictions." The authors of a 1746 inscription and the 1750 gazetteer that copies it cite Song Na and ask: if the facts were so unclear four hundred years ago, how can they be proven or disproven now? In the history of this cult, the Qing inscription says, "the branches and vines" are so tangled up that it is hard to figure out. In Qing times, as the Manchu emperors simultaneously challenged and supported older ways of governing (as, for instance, with the policy of "mourning at one's post"), Confucian scholars began to worry about discrepancies in the classics. Seeking to clarify orthodox beliefs, they examined the classic texts with critical scholarly eyes, looking for linguistic anachronisms that might tell which texts had been corrupted and how. In this spirit, the compilers of the 1750 edition of the Jurong county gazetteer gave an account of the connection of the Jurong Zhangs with the regional cult of Cishan that employs critical readings and textual tradition to set aside much of the historical evidence while preserving local pride.

The Qing authors present themselves as scholars out to debunk ignorant folk-tales, taking a skeptical stance that handily permits these Jurong men to dismiss the well-documented tradition that Cishan was named Zhang Bo and (more importantly) that he came from the Huzhou area and settled in Guangde. Further explaining away the local tendency to consider this god a member of the imperial family, and insisting that no Confucian scholar would pass on such a story, they write instead, in an anthropological vein, that the god is one of those common in the South, who have been worshipped locally since time immemorial and whose true origins are unknown. In fact, they say, he is the oldest deity in Jurong, coeval with the county itself, and supported by all the communities (*she* 社) of Jurong together, who had built and in 1746 rebuilt his temple. Now setting aside their skepticism about the fog of antiquity, the gazetteer compilers report that the god was originally a Jurong native surnamed Zhang, whose parents lived outside the south gate and had their tomb there; namely, the current Zhang family temple in the southern suburb.[29] The antiquity of this Zhang god and his family is reflected in the saying, quoted to me with pride by Zhang Qingwen, that "First there were the Yitai Zhang, then there was Jurong city."[30]

The Qianlong writers argued that the human life of the Zhang god could not be recovered, but they did not doubt the reality of the deity's power. The twin jades of popular worship and imperial honors would not have been the deity's for so long, they say, had he not consistently responded to requests for help. Apart from his ability to bring rain, they recorded two instances of his efficacy. The first was the deity's smile in answer to Taizu's request for a sign, which showed the god's numinous power. Second, the many Zhangs living in front of the Zhang family temple, the original location of Cishan's temple, are all the god's posterity. When the farming women of the village go out into the fields, they leave their babies in the god's temple, bowing to him to ask him to protect them until they return. No baby has ever been lost. These two items, the writers conclude, show the Zhang god's numinous power in blessing the family and protecting the nation or dynasty (*guo* 國).[31]

Just as Taizu had simultaneously rejected and accepted the melons, so the Qianlong compilers both cast scorn on and recorded local stories to elevate Cishan as a local Jurong god. The Jurong Zhang god had smiled on the future Ming founder and had received an imperial temple in return. But he was never too high and mighty to look after the babies of his descendants, who lived clustered around him. In this double duty, the Zhang god was like his descendants, all the way down to Zhang Jian. The family motto on the pillars of one of the Yitai Zhang ancestral halls, imperfectly recalled by Lujiang village head Zhang Yuansheng in 2004, expressed the double virtue of the Zhangs, serving state and family:

> In the Jin dynasty, loyal ministers and sons; 晉朝忠臣子
> In the Tang period, a filial son's family. 唐代孝子家[32]

In response to the double melons in 1372, Taizu wrote: "Whatever lucky omens arise within a piece of land of several feet, several tens of inches, or several *mou*, they are only lucky for him who owns and manages it." This concession of heavenly approbation was not merely theoretical. Nor did Zhang Guan need it to hold moral authority in his native place. A short distance from Guan's own grave mound was that of the Tang-period filial exemplar Zhang Changwei (see p. 74), who had called forth numinous fungus and white crows, and for whom imperial patronage confirmed honor, as much as conferring it. The site came to double as a Zhang ancestral temple. A little further south was another Zhang ancestral temple, which doubled as the home temple (in the minds of Jurong people) of a powerful regional god, the most ancient deity of Jurong, a deity who for centuries had patronized not only his own Zhang descendants, but all of Fuzuo district, indeed all of Jurong county; a deity whose power reached beyond his native place to the whole Jiangnan area and as far as Guizhou; a deity who had in fact patronized the Ming founder himself—an upstart from a no-account Jurong family—when his future was still uncertain.

Chapter VI

Retelling the Melon Story

The universe is made of stories, not of atoms.

Muriel Rukeyser

When Taizu appropriated the site of a temple in the Purple Hills for his tomb complex, the temple moved to nearby Linggu park. There the Jade Belt Bridge, whose name seems to make sense as a simple description, curves over a stream. One day, as Zhu Yuanzhang crossed the bridge, one of the eighty-two ginkgo trees nearby (gone now) smiled at him slightly. (So the sign informs the tourist today.) Pleased, he gave it the title "Tree King." Suddenly, a branch of green leaves on the tree turned bright yellow, as ginkgos do in the fall. Taizu laughed and said: "I enfeoff you as the Tree King and as soon as you receive the mandate you put on [imperial] yellow dragon robes!?" And he gave the tree a jade belt to girdle the "robes."

That such a story is invented to explain one small bridge tells us something about the tireless way people create meanings for the objects around them. Not everyone in Ming China could read, but everyone could listen to stories and moral lessons read or told, watch operas performed at festivals celebrating deities' birthdays, and see the murals and statues in temples. When they thought about themselves, they drew on the great warehouse of tradition to place themselves in these cultural contexts, and they read the present in terms of the past, whether fact or fable. As Peter H. Lee has written,

> The poet's task was to transmit living tradition by a new arrangement of old material, thus lending added significance to the tradition. The poet's (or singer's) countless variations on the same theme were a source of pleasure and a compliment to the memory of listeners, who were quick to recognize allusions to earlier versions, to see the efficacy of the old in the new context, and to feel the aesthetic response his invention aroused.[1]

70

Hok-lam Chan has shown that Ming historical writing consciously enhanced Taizu's "mystique" by reworking the official and popular legends about him, some of which he himself had created. Whereas historical events could be reworked for "propaganda and persuasion," Chan argues that the process also shows how people adopted and changed the stories themselves, in fiction, drama, oral storytelling, and songs.[2]

Tao Kai and the ministers had focused on the melon fruits, but the melon or gourd plant itself was just as important as a cultural artifact. Like gardens, which were carefully arranged for aesthetic enjoyment but also produced crops that could be eaten or sold, the melon vine was both prosaic and poetical. One Ming gentryman wrote:

> Melon vines in the garden, long bedraggled in the cold;
> the yam vines too have collapsed since the coming of fall.
> A light rain has wet the dark path below the flowers;
> a passing cloud has shaded over the bamboo-fringed pond.[3]

The locus classicus for the *gua* vines is the classic *Book of Songs*, the collection of songs from the Shang and Zhou periods about farming and gathering, love and betrayal, war and politics, and ritual. The songs were part of the cultural repertoire of Chinese people at every social level and were interpreted by scholars as moral and political messages. The great nineteenth-century Protestant missionary translator James Legge renders the verse "Mianmian guadie" (綿綿瓜瓞) as:

> In long trains ever increasing grow the gourds.
> When [our] people first sprang
> From the country about the Ts'eu and Ts'eih,
> The ancient duke T'an-foo
> Made for them houses and caves,
> Ere they had yet any houses.[4]

The Song Neo-Confucian Zhu Xi's commentary, which every Ming literatus studied, explains: the vine starts out small and spreads and grows unbrokenly, just as the people of the Zhou dynasty began in one small area and spread out under the guidance of their leaders. Song Lian had this poem in mind when he interpreted the melon omen in terms of the long vines and luxuriant leaves signaling for

Taizu "the blessing of sagely sons and divine grandsons enjoying numberless years forever."

But the association of *gua* plants with, as Peter Lee sums it up, "family descent, its unbroken line and future continuity, in short, the greatness of royal works"[5] was itself an appropriation of a popular celebration of fertility. Not only the luxuriant vines, but also the many seeds of the melon/gourd had long signified fertility. Archaeologists have found many clay vessels in the shape of gourds from about five thousand years ago, before dynastic rule, and the *Book of Songs* includes expressions of satisfaction with a good harvest also connected with harvest festivals.[6] The spreading melon vine could represent the prosperity of any lineage, not just the royal house. The ode's opening was quoted in the Yitai Zhang genealogy, for instance.[7] The *gua* had a double life. It represented both popular and royal prosperity, and its appropriation for the latter meaning never erased the former.

In Living Memory

Like some twentieth-century intellectuals, Taizu idealized the farming folk, placing his faith in them. He hoped that by speaking to ordinary people directly he could morally renovate society from the bottom upward. He issued many public texts, from early proclamations like the one issued to Jurong on lucky grain to a series of dramatic and grisly anecdotes called the *Da Gao* in the 1380s, which everyone was supposed to own and memorize, to the *Placard of People's Instructions* issued toward the end of his life. The *Placard* set up a system of "village elders" to settle disputes, gather men drafted for corvée labor and military duty, oversee irrigation works, get lazy farmers up in the morning, and keep an eye on officials and subjects alike. It ordered villagers to diligently cultivate mulberry trees to feed silkworms, study the *Da Gao*, carry out the community libation ceremony and sacrifices to the local gods of soil and grain, guide one another morally, and help one another financially. Further, each village was to hire an old or disabled person to walk through the village, guided by a child, clanging a copper bell with a wooden clapper. "Let them shout loudly so that everyone can hear, urging people to do good and not violate the law. Their message is: 'Be filial to your parents, respect seniors, maintain harmony with neighbors, instruct and discipline sons and grandsons, live and work in peace and contentment, do no wrongful acts.' This shall be done six times each month."[8] These "Six Maxims" were expanded to sixteen articles in the Qing *Sacred Edict* and promulgated publicly through texts, lectures, and dramatic readings throughout the land.[9] Just as officials exhorted the emperor to be good, so the ruler and officials exhorted the people.

In the Ming period, the last major imperial attempt at empire-wide moral exhortation came in the 1440s. The *Book of the Five Relationships* (*Wulun shu*) was an imperial compilation of moral exemplars, distributed to every county. Begun under the Xuande emperor in imitation of an elegant, illustrated Korean printed book, it included an account of the melon audience among other imperial receptions of omens. The 1447 edition of the *Book of the Five Relationships*, held in the Harvard-Yenching library, is about 16 inches tall and 9 inches wide: large enough to be impressive, but small enough to be comfortable for reading. The characters are beautifully carved, big and clear, and the edition was intended to be read, not just owned, because it was punctuated at the time of carving. If a book as a material object may be said to have a character (which is easy to doubt until one holds it in one's hands), this one gives an impression of majesty earnestly and hopefully teaching the reader. The throne presents to the reading public the incident of the melons, along with other stories, as a fruition of the ideal relationship between those dual parts of the state, ruler and minister.[10]

In the *Book of the Five Relationships*, the 1372 melon story falls under the category "Way of the ruler—good speech—the virtue of modesty." This category gives examples from antiquity through the Yongle reign of monarchs who rejected flattery. Tang Taizong (r. 627–649) pointed out that his reign was not over yet: depending on what happened, later generations might laugh at him for permitting the transmission of an essay about him called "On Sagely Virtue." Two Han emperors went so far as to forbid the presentation of omens and the "high-sounding drivel" that accompanied them. Taizu's anti-omen stance, therefore, had precedents, yet none of the earlier objections is quite like his. The earlier monarchs did not question the possibility that imperial virtue might bring forth omens, nor did they argue that the omens responded to someone else's virtue. The *Book of the Five Relationships* text adopts almost wholesale the *Veritable Records* account of the 1372 conversation. It omits the last sentence about how kingly omens do not appear in trivial things, the cash reward, and the ode blessing Zhang Guan.[11] The point is Taizu's appropriate modesty. Over Taizu's own protests, the court accepted the melon omen and used it for imperial propaganda and moral exhortation. The court text was then re-appropriated by the locality—the account of the melon audience in the 1496 Jurong gazetteer is copied directly from *The Book of the Five Relationships*, and the ode Taizu wrote is included too. The troubling aftermath is largely elided.[12] The gazetteer did report the executions and exile, in the context of praise for the Zhang women's virtue. It was not politic to dwell on Taizu's ingratitude and injustice to the Zhang brothers, but one poem in the 1496 gazetteer may express sorrow about it indirectly. It is one of a set of four poems by different men called "Righteous Platform, Autumn Moon," referring to the monument for Zhang Changwei, the Tang filial son, which according to the Yitai Zhang genealogy had become a famous scenic spot. The author, Zhang Hui 張憓 (not the magistrate), was probably kin to Zhang Guan: he was a Zhang of the city and shared a radical in his name with Zhang Jian's sons, who were roughly his age.[13]

In the south of Juqu city [i.e., Jurong] is a relic of the past:
Mr. Zhang, those years, was praised for his upright virtue.
The massed bamboos weep dew, the autumn grasses are wild;
The domed gravestone braves the rain, lichen in the scars of erosion.
From time to time I hear a vast wind, scattering heaven's incense;
Momentarily I glimpse the icy wheel [of the moon], rolling empty jade.
Pacing, I don't realize the night is already late;
Circling the trees, the calling birds' sound is truly anxious.[14]

In Zhang Hui's poem, as in omen theory, nature responds to human sincerity—the bamboos weep, the birds are anxious. Zhang's images may allude to a famous Tang poem that begins with the term *jia gua*, the term used to describe Zhang Guan's "auspicious melons." In the Tang poem, however, the "fine melon" (as James Liu translates it) refers to a beautiful girl, lost to the poet Li Shangyin when she was married off to a powerful man.

The fine melon [*jia gua*] stretches its long tendrils;
Its green jade freezes in the cold water.

Though its five colors shine at Eastern Mound (Dongling),
How can one bear to bite its fragrant flesh?[15]

Zhang Hui, who like all literati would have memorized hundreds of
poems, brings Li's Shangyin's poem to the reader's mind through a
series of images and puns. Zhang Hui's "icy jade wheel" recalls Li's
"jade freezing in cold water." His "incense" recalls the "fragrant flesh."
Hui's "autumn grasses" puns on a second meaning of Li's *han jiang*;
in addition to meaning "cold water," it is a kind of grass. "Five Colors"
and "Eastern Mound" are both names for a famous kind of melon.[16]
But "Eastern Mound" also suggests a grave, like the Yitai, the Righteous Platform of Changwei where the poem was composed, and the
Yilong, the Righteous Mound, where the brothers Guan and Qian
were buried. Perhaps Zhang Hui, standing among Zhang graves on a
cold autumn night, alluded to this famous poem to evoke Guan's
offering and execution.

Or is it just that I myself am obsessed with the story? All other
surviving mid-Ming texts on the incidents find a way to reconcile
the throne with the local family. They do so through the medium of
the successful and filial grandson Zhang Jian. For instance, Ni Qian's
epitaph for Zhang Yi, written at his death in about 1456, speaks of
the family's sufferings in order to praise Yi for rising above them.

> Early in the Hongwu period, the family garden once
> grew auspicious melons, one stem, a pair of fruits. [Zhang
> Guan] presented them to High Emperor Taizu, who
> personally made an ode to praise them and ordered
> history official Song Lian to make a hymn. Everyone said
> that [the melons] were the vessel [or concentration] of
> goodness and congratulation. Later, they vindicated
> [Yi's] Uncle Gugong's unjust treatment at court. Because
> of the unjust deaths, the family moved to Chongshan.[17]

In this account, Tao Kai and the other ministers are gone. Only
Song Lian remains, because of the tribute he was ordered to pay
to Zhang Guan. The enthusiasm with which Zhang Guan was
welcomed home from the capital comes through, as do the hopes
for continued blessings from the association with the throne. The
destruction of those hopes is clear too: the court is blamed for
executing the innocent.

Ni goes so far as to suggest that the family's disasters could bring on a crisis of faith, a fear that there was no underlying order assuring justice and expressed in the signs of Heaven and Earth.

> Alas! The *Odes* speak of the long unbroken *gua* vines, meaning the birth of the Zhou people, from small to large. Now, one stalk with two fruits, how could it not be a lucky sign of sons and grandsons greatly ramifying? But to the contrary, [the family] met with a great fall. [One might] wonder whether this was an omen with no response. Today we observe that Mr. Zhang left home but returned again, personally received the grace of "enfeoffment" [i.e., an honorary title], and enjoyed a long life. And [we observe] his sons and grandsons worthily flourishing, the mass of the clan all together more than eight hundred people eating together. From this we can know the reach of this auspicious omen. It is expressed in the decline midway and announced in the final good fortune. It was all foreordained. Heaven's way does not err; how could one not believe in it?[18]

In Ni's interpretation, the omen was for the family. The melons were vessels condensing the virtue of the family, and the vines, despite their canonical interpretation association with the expansion of the ancient Zhou state, foreshadowed the many sons and grandsons of Zhang Guan's son. Guan's melons had nothing to do with the emperor or the realm. Moreover, despite the original disaster, the omen was proved correct. The crisis of faith potentially brought on by its apparent error is resolved by Zhang Yi's long life, his return home surrounded by descendants, and by the title Zhang Jian won for him. The funerary ode Ni also contributed further expresses that it was not only the Zhang family who were seemingly betrayed and then redeemed, but also Jurong county itself—Jurong whose lofty mountains and flourishing *qi* produced both remarkable melons and remarkable people. Guan's virtue and the double melons, Yi's well-regulated family, and Jian's filiality and dedication to public service all had roots nourished in rich soil.

So once Jian had passed the metropolitan examination in 1439, and had been recognized for his filial mourning after his mother's death in 1443, there were ways to tell the melon story and even admit to the emperor's transgression of justice without danger: the conflict had been resolved. The audience was included in the *Book of the Five Relationships* and then caught the imagination of some mid-Ming literati. One of the compilers of the *Book of the Five Relationships*, Liu Yan 劉儼 (1394–1457), wrote "Auspicious Melon Poem," which was included in the 1496 Jurong gazetteer.

The emperor received the Mandate,
standardizing axles and writing in a great unity.
Thus the people increased,
and doubled grain attended the farmer.
Who protected it? Who cut [or "administered"] it?
North and South China rose together.
The transformation extended to all things,
each with its color, each in its shape.
A melon had auspicious fruit,
sharing a stalk, of admirable appearance [or "of flourishing (Ju)rong"].
If one looks at other, common produce,
it is really very different.
Round as matched jades,
hard as green jades.
If one compared their size–
far larger than the duckweed.
The prefect presented them to the emperor;
The emperor said: "It is *you* [who] can [take the credit]. (*er neng*)
The response is to the commoner.
His presentation shows his sincerity.
From this time on,
Heaven will be pure, Earth will be peaceful;
and also Mr. Zhang
will have grandsons in the public service,
for a hundred generations carrying on his line,
if not scholars, then farmers."[19]

This is a reasonably accurate précis of some of what Taizu wrote (and possibly said). Like the emperor's ode, Liu's poem refers to the auspicious duckweed fruit seen by the King of Chu. The peculiar phrase *er neng* 爾能 comes from Taizu's rhetorical question *Zhen he you neng* 朕何有能 "How can I [claim to] have any ability?" But while adopting some of Taizu's phrases Liu rejects his complex arguments. Taizu had directed his good wishes for harmony to the farmer's family, saying "I wish you in every generation a harmonious family and a peaceful household" (*Jia he hu ning* 家和戶寧). In Liu's poem, the emperor wishes more generally, "From this time on, Heaven pure, Earth peaceful" (*Qian qing kun ning* 乾清坤寧), a phrase more closely related to the opening lines of Song Lian's hymn:

> Heaven's way is filled with purity;
> Earth upholds it using tranquility.
> Protected and joined in great harmony,
> They bring forth blessings and good omens.[20]

Moreover, Liu alters Taizu's final good wishes for Zhang by making specific the general reference to the feudal lords and by skipping the (as it had turned out) unlucky generation of Zhang's sons, to promise a grandson in office. The emperor, in this version, has predicted Zhang Jian's success. Similarly, the famous mid-Ming philosopher and scholar Xue Xuan (1392–1464) briefly recounts the presentation of the melons. He dwells on the fact that Taizu himself wrote an ode specifically to disclaim responsibility for the good omen and to attribute it to the farmer, despite the views of the Rites officials. He praises Taizu for surpassing all former rulers by not falling prey to the flattery and delusion of good omens, but he points out that in fact, at the time, yin and yang *had* been coming in proper sequence and harvested grain *had* been piling up. The melons (despite Taizu's protestations) really *did* illustrate and spring from an era of great peace. Moreover, the founder's "sagely sons and divine grandsons" are continuing on and on for "a million ten-thousand years": Is this not one of the things the auspicious melons presaged? But that is not all. The lineage of Zhang Guan has also gradually flourished and spread, and his grandson is now a censor, so "the Sagely Progenitor's comment that 'vegetable omens produced in that ground respond only to the people of that ground' is also amply proved."[21]

Writing like this praised Zhang Jian and the dynasty simultaneously. Both, after all, were now involved in the same enterprise of running the state. Papering over the little unpleasantness that had befallen Jian's grandfather and great-uncle, and the exile of his father, one could present the Ming founder (or his descendants) and the official (or his grandfather Guan) as both congratulated by the melons. After the flirtation of the Jurong god's smile and the broken pledge of the double melons, the bond between the Zhang and Zhu families had been finally solemnized when Jian earned a *jinshi* degree and became a well-respected official. These texts celebrate the reconciliation, which wove together two strands in the cloth of the empire. An intriguing poem in the gazetteer represents this balance quite clearly. Wu Jie 吳節 (1397–1481), another contemporary of Jian, also wrote about the melons. The whole form of the poem represents the duality of the melons and their message. Most lines use reduplication or repetition, and its two parallel stanzas, most unusually, are printed in the 1750 gazetteer on two lines to emphasize that formal structure, instead of wrapping around (since most Chinese poems have a predictable number of syllables per line, line breaks are unnecessary).

> ah, melon, your seedling
> longer, longer; more, more
> nourish it, cultivate it
> so: double! so: ripen!

> oh, melons, your oddness
> two *qi*s marvelously congealed
> show forth emperor's mandate
> ah, fortunate! ah, propitious![22]

The first stanza speaks of the melon plant's natural growth and the farmer's work; the second speaks of how yin and yang combine in the strangeness of double melons to bear witness to the Mandate of Heaven. Wu Jie balances the claims made to the melons for Zhang Guan and Taizu.

Wu Jie and Liu Yan were Zhang Jian's contemporaries, and they probably knew him personally. In fact, Zhang Jian was not only a passive vessel for textual reconciliation. Xue Xuan's account, given above, is from a postface he wrote to a work that probably no longer exists called *Jia gua ji* 嘉瓜集, "Collection on Auspicious Melons." After giving Taizu credit for essentially foreseeing Jian's success and heaping additional praise on the dynasty for its guidance and on Zhang Jian for following it, Xue continues:

> But though wealth may be great, what can be stored up
> has its limits. If we compare it with a well, if you do not
> dig very deep, it will dry up. How can you hold on to
> good fortune? His Honor the Censor [Zhang Jian] there-
> fore extracted the account of the auspicious melons from
> the *Book of the Five Relationships*, and also the traditions

as handed down by the family, and arranged them into a collection. The famous scholar-gentrymen all contributed pieces and also asked me to say something, so I have written this postface.[23]

Zhang Jian, in other words, was actively soliciting contributions to his family's fund of virtue and honor, presented here as identical or interchangeable, just like a family's capital in silver. Another prominent official of the time, Li Ling, wrote a preface and long poem at Jian's request.[24] It is likely that the poems by Liu Yan and Wu Jie were also requested for the project, probably some time around 1460 (between Zhang Yi's death and Xue Xuan's). Although he apparently never published them, Zhang Jian gathered all these contributions into a textual treasure chest.

Later Retellings

During Zhang Jian's lifetime, and for some time thereafter, his standing as a well-known official kept the tone respectful when the melon story was told. But once Jian died, leaving no successors in office, the family tended to fade from the story again, or even to look bad. Writers who did not know Jian personally used the story to comment on their times or criticize their contemporaries. Plot and phrasings moved from one text to another, but shifting emphases and different juxtapositions reveal each author's judgment on the events and his own contemporary concerns.

In a history of the Hanlin Academy, the capital's think tank, Huang Zuo (1490–1566) includes a summary of Song Lian's piece.

In the fifth year, sixth month, the garden of a Jurong county commoner, Zhang Guan, produced auspicious melons, a pair of fruits sharing a single stalk, round as matched jades. Minister of Rites Tao Kai presented them as a contribution. [The emperor] ordered them put in the Qianqing palace. The next day he offered them in the Imperial Ancestral Temple. Song Lian contributed the "Hymn on Auspicious Melons."[25]

Huang mentions Zhang Guan but gives Minister Tao Kai a central role as having "presented [the melons] as a contribution" (*feng zhi yi xian* 奉之以獻). Ignoring the comments of the other ministers and even Song Lian's own views, he highlights Hanlin alumnus Song's contribution (*xian* 獻) of a hymn, and his poetic description of the melons as "a pair of fruits sharing a single stalk, round as matched jades."[26] The beauty of the poetry must match that of the melons, because the point is not the physical omen itself, but rather the text that it occasioned. Both text and melons are contributions from minister to emperor. Huang Zuo lists several other omens commemorated by members of the Hanlin Academy, dwelling on the presentation of the texts, the happiness with which the early Ming emperors received them, and further exchanges of goodwill that resulted. Huang Zuo refuses to remember Taizu's and Yongle's massacres, their clashes with officials.

What lies behind Huang Zuo's idealization of the relation between Taizu and his ministers was perhaps the greatest clash between throne and bureaucracy in Ming history. In the 1520s, just as Huang began his career, the "Great Ritual Controversy" rocked the state. Taizu's great-great-great-great-great-grandson the Zhengde emperor had died with no heir. His cousin enthroned as the Jiajing emperor fought bitterly—and ultimately successfully—with the scholar-officials and literati out of office for the right to posthumously dub his own father a "former emperor." Many officials claimed that Taizu's rules of imperial descent by primogeniture required him, instead, to adopt a previous emperor as his father. They accused him of a narrow personal filiality that threatened the whole Ming enterprise by undermining public ritual distinctions and categorizations.[27] John Dardess suggests that in this view, the "private family and the public realm [were] wholly separate and indeed incommensurable ritual spheres."[28] Even the fundamental principles of the "Great Learning" seem open to debate: as Irene Bloom writes of the Confucian tradition, "Within the large tent that is sometimes labeled 'orthodoxy,' there was room for a wide variety of attitudes and opinions."[29]

Some officials, drawing in part on an influential new form of Neo-Confucianism that focused on human emotion, supported the iron-willed Jiajing emperor's view of things and rose in rank accordingly. Those who insisted on displaying their own understanding of the emperor's family and public duties paid dearly: they were demoted, removed from office, imprisoned, exiled, beaten until they were permanently crippled, and even flogged to death. Huang Zuo, author of the Hanlin Academy history, had not been deeply involved in the Great Ritual Controversy but had sided against the emperor. In 1530, he filially sped home without permission upon learning that his mother was ill and was dismissed from office by an angry Jiajing emperor on grounds of disrespect to the throne. Amid these clashes among succession rules, filial piety, loyalty, and family pride, Huang Zuo used the melon incident and other stories to paint the early Ming court as, in Peter Ditmanson's words, "a seamless locus of moral order and authority."[30] Covering up the hostility between officials and the Ming founder, Huang idealized the early Ming ruler-minister relationship to rebuke his own time, when a pig-headed ruler fought with officials who demonstrated *en masse* against his decision.

A far more colorful version of the story was given by Shen Defu (1578–1642), writing in the late Ming period, perhaps around 1615. Shen also exalts the Ming founder, this time at the expense of Zhang Guan. To Tao Kai's presentation of the melons, Shen has Taizu respond:

> "Vegetable omens, like lucky grain with joined heads, interlocked trees or trees growing together, grain with two heads, melons on the same stalk—these all are. You take them as returning my virtue. I am not virtuous and dare not presume. Moreover, vegetable omens also respond only to the person on whose ground they grew. What do they have to do with me?"[31]

The wording shows that Shen Defu drew on a number of sources to create his own interpretation. For instance, he misrepresents the point of Taizu's list of vegetable omens just as Xie Jin did in the *Veritable Records*, but he must have also seen Taizu's own essay since he includes trees that grow together, which Xie omits. The farmer's name and later fate must have come from other sources. For Shen continues:

> [The emperor] just gave the commoner 1,200 cash and that was it. The history does not report the commoner's name. Note: the commoner was called Zhang Guan. A short time after he produced the melons, elder and younger brother were implicated in a crime and both were beheaded in the marketplace. Taizu's lofty outlook

does not need to be pointed out; it is as if he had the
wisdom to foresee the future of the case! Probably the
joined-stalk [melons] were the image of the pair of
severed heads.[32]

Shen dramatically likens the two round melons to the severed heads
of the unfortunate brothers, perhaps grasped together by their long
hair. In earlier treatments Taizu and Zhang Guan had interacted
indirectly, through at least Tao Kai and sometimes several layers of
officials. But here, Taizu is able to see directly into Zhang Guan's
character. "Men and melons are hard to know," says Poor Richard—
but not for the wise Ming founder, who recognized that the brothers
were scoundrels.

Showing quite clearly that Ming people sometimes interpreted
anomalies as omens referring to individual subjects, Shen details
recent "lucky omens" that came just before disaster. In 1530, auspicious double lotus blooms grew on the pond of a Mr. Yang, who
died of an ulcer on his back that same year. In 1604, the gentry wrote
poems praising seven lotus blooms that grew from one stalk in the
Huguang governor's mansion. When the governor was promoted
people said there was a connection, but he died an unnatural death
in a rebellion a few months later. The Jiajing emperor himself
accepted a double melon omen presented by Hou Tingxun in 1531
with credulous excitement, personally presenting Hou's drawing or
the melons themselves in the audience hall. Shen notes that the
double melons were taken as heralding the birth of the heir apparent
a year later. But after only a month, the little prince died. So much
for auspiciousness![33] Shen contrasts Taizu's wise rejection of the
1372 "omen" with the Jiajing emperor's credulity. Reporting Taizu's
view that anomalies may have local meaning partially undercuts
Shen's praise of the founder, but the foolishness shared by Jiajing
and his subjects is the real point.

In the late Ming period, a number of histories of the dynasty
included the melon audience without Zhang Guan's later fate. The
omen served as a comment on different aspects of history and governance, depending on its placement and what was omitted or
selected around it. Zhu Guozhen, for instance, more or less follows
the *Veritable Records* version of the audience in the annals of his
history, but he also briefly mentions the audience in his biography of Tao Kai, where he follows it immediately with Tao Kai's

proferring a more acceptable form of flattery—namely the suggestion that the Ming dynasty should follow precedent by compiling a
Huiyao to record its institutions.[34] Another late Ming work, an annal-
istic chronicle with just a few items per year, the *Mingji biannian*
seems to take its cue from Song Lian as it juxtaposes military campaigns with the omen. Hongwu 5 (1372), the fifth year of the Hongwu
reign, begins with General Xu Da and others campaigning in the
desert after a speech by the emperor about the historic mission of
defeating the Mongols. Next comes the presentation of auspicious
melons by a commoner from Jurong, to which the emperor responds:
"If times are peaceful and harvests are plentiful, that is a sign of
kingliness. Objects are not."[35] Song's triumphal tone is lost. The
compiler may have been anxious about the threat from the north-
eastern Manchu-Mongol forces who would ultimately replace the
Ming dynasty with the Qing dynasty.

A final late Ming example is the item in a 1620 history headed
"Jurong county presents auspicious melons":

> A Jurong commoner presented two melons on the same
> stalk. The Secretariat led the hundred officials to con-
> gratulate. Tao Kai said, "Jurong is Your Majesty's ances-
> tral home. The good omen of paired melons joined at the
> stalk has only appeared there. This is really highly fortu-
> nate!" The emperor said, "I am not virtuous. How dare
> I presume [*He gan dang* 何敢當]? Moreover, vegetable
> omens produced in a certain place only respond to the
> people of that place. What do they have to do with me?
> If throughout the space between heaven and earth times
> are peaceful and harvests abundant, then that is 'highly
> fortunate!' Not in trivial things!" He rewarded the com-
> moner and sent him away.[36]

Here Tao Kai seems a mere flatterer, and the commoner seems to
have been after more than a cash reward. The subtle conflicts and
manipulations of the long early Ming treatments are lost. This
account is also the only one to say that the hundred officials came
to "congratulate," which had by the time of writing become the
standard locution in reports of later Ming presentations of auspicious
vegetables, whether the officials were rebuked by the throne for
flattery or folly (as they usually did until the Jiajing period) or
not. Even as Taizu's extraordinary argument is retained, the incident is assimilated to later, less loaded, more standardized omen

presentations. By the time it was incorporated into the popular encyclopedia *Xu wenxian tongkao*,[37] the living memory of both Taizu and the Zhang family had receded completely, specific details had been lost, and the story's emotional weight had diminished.

Into the New Millennium . . .

Did the story stay alive in Jurong? The late twentieth-century Jurong antiquarian Cheng Zunping mentions the melon story twice, once to connect his county with the great Chinese past, and once to reinforce its claim to Ming Taizu. In the summer of Ming Hongwu 5, he writes, the garden of "our county's Zhang Guan" produced auspicious melons. After quoting (without attribution) Song Lian's poetic description of the melons, he notes that double melons have appeared in "our country" since the Han and Tang dynasties and have been presented to rulers as good omens.[38] Cheng's double self-identification as a Jurong person and an heir to the great tradition of China would have made sense to Zhang Jian. In the next item, Zhang Guan has already lost his name; only his status as a Jurong person matters. Cheng quotes Tao Kai telling Taizu that Jurong is his ancestral home and comments that this proves that it was so, or how would Tao have dared to say so to the emperor's face? Here, as in the ministers' original explanation of the melons, the melons' only function is to show something about the Ming founder—whom, even after several revolutions, the residents of Jurong still wish to claim.[39]

A collection of "folk-tales" made in the late twentieth century also includes a version of the story, called "Not Believing in 'Auspicious Melons.'"

> In Hongwu 5 of the Ming dynasty (1372), in summer, Minister of Rites Tao Kai suddenly with great excitement used a black lacquer dish engraved with dragons to present to Zhu Yuanzhang a pair of watermelons and repeated over and over that they were "rare treasures."
> Zhu Yuanzhang felt very perplexed. "Ailiaoya! Aren't you just giving me two ordinary watermelons? To eat them is no big deal, not to eat them would be a bit of a waste, what's so rare about them?" Tao Kao knelt and memorialized: "Your Majesty absolutely should not despise this pair of melons! What's rare about them is that

they share a stalk!" Zhu Yuanzhang looked at them again more closely, and really there was no mistake—the two watermelons really had grown from the same stalk of a melon vine. He involuntarily smiled and said, "Hmm! How interesting, I have lived for several decades, and this is really the first time I've seen this!" Tao Kai complacently stood up, saying: "Your Majesty, this kind of same-stalk melon the ancients called 'auspicious melons.' They are a kind of rarely found lucky omen. These were sent in by a pair of brothers from Jurong; it is truly extraordinary!"

When Zhu Yuanzhang heard what Tao Kai said, he felt even more confused. "Tut! Why is it so extraordinary that some Jurong folk sent in 'auspicious melons'?" "Because Jurong is where Your Majesty's ancestors were from! So now, these auspicious melons also growing in Jurong, isn't that really a pretty big lucky omen? It's just because Your Majesty's virtuous government moves Heaven and Earth that Jurong produced this treasure. Your minister thinks they must mean that Your Majesty's state will never change in a thousand autumns and ten thousand generations!" Zhu Yuanzhang, when he heard this, finally understood: You, Tao Kai, have been gabbing at me for so long just because you wanted to use this pair of melons to give me the old soft soap!

At this time Zhu Yuanzhang had not been emperor for long, and his head was still pretty clear, so he criticized Tao Kai not a bit politely: "When I was little, I didn't even have rice to eat, and a good many of my relatives died of hunger. At that time, I also heard of many heads of grain growing on one stalk, flowers that grew together and such stories. If you say that their appearance portends good for the empire, then how could there have been people starving to death? How could there have been people who rebelled because they had no way to survive? You take the appearance of this pair of 'auspicious melons' as redounding to my virtuous government; the interpretation is really too strained and arbitrary! I can figure out for myself how great my meritorious virtue is! And furthermore, if the auspicious melons really are a lucky omen, even so they can only apply to the Jurong men personally. What do they have to do with me?"

To this barrage of speech, Tao Kai had not a word to say in reply.

In the end, the story continues, Taizu was only willing to have Tao give those who had presented the melons 120 cash to cover their transport costs there and back. Not long after, this pair of brothers who had presented the melons, because they committed a serious crime, both got their heads chopped off by the authorities. Since Taizu in the affair of the "auspicious melons" had true knowledge and clear sight, he avoided becoming a laughingstock.[40]

In this Communist-era version, the focus is on the canny emperor, referred to by his given name. Still close to his proletarian roots, he is able to evade the wiles of the complacent flatterer by out-arguing or out-shouting him. The impure motivations of the unnamed brothers are only hinted at in that they later committed crimes. There is little sympathy for them, even though they were local men; the narrator's sympathies lie with Taizu if anywhere. On the other hand, Tao Kai, not the brothers, is the real target of the story, and one could suggest parallels to common understandings of the Maoist era: the supreme leader who early on is still clear-headed, close to the people, and focused on practical problems; the hanger-on overly confident of his ability to manipulate the ruler through flattery.

In May, 2004, I visited Jurong county. After several days of collaborative research, I discussed the melon story with my hosts, who had read the folktale version in preparation for my visit. Wen Dezhong, a former high school language teacher working for the Education Office of the Cultural Bureau of Jurong county, first said that in his view, the brothers were approaching Taizu as one would approach a hooligan or gang boss (*liu mang*) with whom one had a remote connection: flattering him in hopes of getting some kind of payoff. Zhai Zhonghua, the head of the Jurong Museum, more or less concurred. He thought that Zhang Guan wanted to be appointed to office. Then I explained another facet of the story as I saw it: that the Zhangs were honored in Jurong, whereas the Zhus had been nobodies; that the Zhangs were perhaps unlikely to have completely changed their view of the families' respective social standings even when Zhu was on the throne; that their presentation of the melons perhaps did not mean that they really approved of the new ruler. Mr. Wen eagerly responded that this angle made sense to him. It was, he said, "a Chinese way of thinking"; I should tell the story that way in my book. In Mr. Wen's revised view, Zhang Guan really despised (*kanbuqi* 看不起) Zhu Yuanzhang, but since he had become emperor,

Guan presented the melons to show that we, of the old home town, condescend to approve (*peifu* 佩服) you. To his surprise, Guan found that it was not the old Zhu Yuanzhang, now that he was emperor. Zhu in fact was able to despise Zhang Guan and gave him a little money just to demonstrate his disdain. Later, Zhu took advantage of some excuse to get him executed. Whether or not Mr. Wen's interpretation closely matches Taizu's own account, it makes sense in light of the way relations with powerful people in the Communist era worked.

Mr. Wen's and Mr. Zhai's responses, as well as mine, show that the story of the auspicious melons is still generating new interpretations some six hundred years after the brothers were buried in the Righteous Mound. Writing history is like making a collage: we work with fragments of the creations of others. Each historian becomes part of the story. An item in the June 2004 edition of a journal called *Jiangxi Local Gazetteers* retells the story of the melons and reprints Taizu's ode. The author comments that from this we can see that although Zhu Yuanzhang had become emperor, his mind was still clear. The short item continues:

> American Ming history expert Shi Shanshan 施珊珊, after hearing this story, was very interested, and many times sent letters and e-mails, and opened relations with the Jurong city government, and even on May 5, 2004, flew to Jurong, browsing through great quantities of local materials; visiting Zhu Yuanzhang's old home . . . ; and looking for the "Righteous Mound" where Zhang Guan and his brother were buried, the Tang dynasty filial son Zhang Changwei's tomb the "Righteous Platform," the protected landmark Zhang ancestral temple, etc., basically figuring out all the related figures and circumstances and the content of the story.[41]

Shi Shanshan is my Chinese name. I myself have now been gathered into the Jurong display cabinet.

In the Taiping Rebellion of the 1850s, in the Japanese invasion of the 1940s, in the "Great Leap Forward" movement of the late 1950s to create communes, and again in the Cultural Revolution in the 1960s and 1970s, Jurong, "the gateway to Nanjing," suffered waves of devastation that cost millions of lives and damaged or destroyed nearly every old building. But even in the early twenty-first century, the past is still remembered and forms part of people's understanding of themselves. After I left, museum head Zhai Zhonghua located part of an old Zhang ancestral temple on what is now called Big South Street, but was once Yitai Street, Righteous Platform Street.[42] Now part of someone's home, the section of ancestral temple is across from the site of the Confucian temple/school complex, once the parental tomb where Zhang Changwei mourned, which now hosts the Huayang Primary School. Although the family is dispersed, ancestral sacrifices had continued into the twentieth century. A seventy-five-year-old Jurong resident named Zhang Caibo recalled that before 1949 there was an ancestral sacrifice every year at about the time of the Qingming grave-sweeping festival by men who called themselves the "Yitai Zhang." Landlord Zhang Caifa, the informant's father Zhang Changyi, and other representatives of Zhang branches in various villages would go to a large paper factory (now a row of small shops) in Jurong to conduct the ceremony under the leadership of lineage head Zhang Yinghuang (whose son studied in the United States before returning to head the government education department).[43] Why a paper factory? Because it was located between Yitai Street and what is now called Culture Alley, right near where the ancestral temple has now been discovered.

Mr. Wen and Mr. Zhai also spoke to a seventy-year-old man named Zhang Renyao 张任尧. He reported that the Yitai Zhang (who adopted that appellation in the mid-Ming) and the Yilong Zhang (the descendents of Zhang Guan) were the same family. They have a story, passed down through a branch called the Chenwu Zhang 陈武张, that when Zhang Guan and his brother had been executed and their bodies were brought home, the family had heads of gold made for them, so that they could be buried whole.[44] The Righteous Mound still existed to the right of South Bridge in about 1900. Of the three steles on it one had been shattered by lightning, and on another not a single character could be distinguished, but Shang Lu's epitaph for Zhang Jian was legible enough for Yang Shiyuan to copy it.[45] Perhaps the brothers still lie there. Perhaps they will be found.[46]

The monuments of the Ming dynastic house have survived. Down the stone face of the fortress guarding the rounded and girdled mound where Taizu lies, the rain has been dripping for so long that stalactites have formed. But the Zhang family too holds its place in history. Some time in the early Ming period, a family that now identifies itself as a branch of the Yitai Zhang built an enormous new living compound with four courtyards in Lujiang village. The middle five rooms, a portion measuring 24 by 11 meters, including the ancestral hall, have been recently identified by the Jurong Museum authorities.[47] This building was so solid and impressive that it was preserved even in the madness of the Cultural Revolution, used for storing tractors. Lujiang village head Zhang Yuansheng told me that on rainy days, when he was young, he and the other children played among the *nanmu* wood pillars of the hall. He remembered noticing that the rain dripped down onto one particular stone, that in fact it had been dripping for so long that it had worn a hole in the stone. In the story of the Zhangs of Jurong, the glorious Ming dynasty was merely an episode.

Conclusion

Movement and Exchange in the Ming Empire

We can now imagine two opposite interpretations of the incident with which we began. In 1372, a simple farmer came to Nanjing, in humble loyalty, with sunburned back, paying homage in the form of "trivial" melons to the virtuous, powerful, Heaven-chosen emperor of all China. Or, twin melons, white-green as jade, were presented to the johnny-jump-up grandson of an impoverished Jurong gold panner by a member of the illustrious, even divine, Jurong Zhang family. Perhaps Zhang Guan offered the melons as a condescending sign of his own, of Jurong's approval of the new ruler, with full consciousness of the Zhangs' social superiority. Perhaps the emperor's response—to praise him, pay him, and send him away—was intended to take him down a peg. It is entirely in keeping with Taizu's paranoid character that he later found such mild rebukes insufficient.

The double melons grown in Zhang Guan's garden in the summer of 1372 were interpreted in various ways. In tracing these interpretations, I see the melons and the texts about them as an example of how the relationship between the court and the localities near and far that made up the Ming empire was mediated by the transfer of people, products, and texts. Some of these transfers—of tax money, of soldiers, of officials—could perhaps be seen as unidirectional, as instruments of imperial exploitation and control and no more. The bricks used to build the platforms, walls, and buildings of the Ming founder's tomb, each stamped with the names of the county where it was made, the supervising official, and sometimes the individual maker, were requisitioned in a standard size from all over the empire, as their different colors attest. But some items were sent up to the court voluntarily, like Zhang Guan's melons. The exchange of texts, products, and people went both ways between court and locality, and that continual shuttling back and forth wove a strong imperial fabric.

91

The capital was one center. But it was not the only one. The Righteous Platform, the temple to Cishan, and the other Zhang graves, including the Righteous Mound, offered a spatial focus for identity and emotional grounding that collapsed eras into one another or at least minimized the years between them. This was not a purely local identity, however, but one that sent tendrils out to courts of various times and places, and to other localities where Jurong men and gods lived and worked. It was not that local knowledge continued independent of the center, because the gazetteers combine locally produced texts on the melon incident with centrally produced texts. In the specifics included in the different versions of the incident, there is a constant give and take among imperially sponsored texts, more private texts associated with them, and texts written by local men in the local context. And writers tell and retell the tale for their own purposes—to exalt and to chastise the Ming founder, Tao Kai, the Zhang brothers, and whatever men and types of their own time those characters can represent.

The Zhang men themselves traveled too. They were claimed as Jurong men, and they were buried in Jurong. Zhang Yi's return home was an important part of his identity, and Zhang Jian's filiality was celebrated in Jurong terms as the auspicious signs he called forth echoed those of the Tang paragon Zhang Changwei. But Zhang Yi spent almost his whole long life in exile and on the road, and Zhang Jian, born in Guizhou, spent his life traveling, to study, to serve in office, to bring his father home, and to mourn. He moved from home to court as a representative of local virtue and of culture and learning that transcended imperial time and imperial legitimacy, and from post to post as a representative of the center.

The constant exchange of products, persons, and texts between center and locality was initiated from both sides, served (but not without risk) the purposes of both sides, and wove the empire together. The imperial attention given Guan's melons, the imperial honors accorded Changwei, the titles given Jian and his parents and wives, the imperial cult of the Zhang god—these increased the Zhangs' local standing. The presentation of the melons, the smile of the Jurong god, the loyal and unflagging service of Jian—these increased the prestige of the throne. It is tempting to come down, finally, on one side or the other—to say that the dynasty finally had the upper hand because of its access to violence and its ability to co-opt talent, or to say that local tradition and the Zhang family outlived the dynasty, or that in Jurong the Zhang god was more honored than the Zhu family. But, however tempting such a final decision appears, it is more honest to present center and locality as inextricably intertwined, shaping each other. Each reader and re-teller of this story must decide whether center and locality in Ming China appear like two rice stalks that have grown together to form one head of grain, or like two melons springing from one stalk.

In Praise of Auspicious Melons

Ming Taizu

Hongwu 5, sixth moon. I was in the Military Hall. The time on the water clock was exactly noon. A palace attendant came to report: Officials of various offices were presenting some matter. Suddenly, the secretary, the military commissioner, and the censors all arrived. I thought, "The business of the dawn audience has been taken care of, so this visit must be to set me straight on how to rule." After a while, the minister of rites, Tao Kai, came forward holding up two melons. At first I only knew there were melons and didn't understand what was up. The minister reported: "The melons grew from the same stalk!" When I heard this, I thought it really strange. I tried asking how this was understood in former dynasties. The group of ministers one after another said, "Several emperors of former dynasties had them, and called them good omens. Now, when Your Majesty is ruling, melons growing from the same stalk have been produced in Jurong. Well, Jurong is the emperor's ancestral home. It goes without saying that this is a good omen!" The group of ministers made pretty speeches like this.

I have heard that "Heaven's *qi* descends; Earth's *qi* rises up. At year-end, we get a good yield; the people bring in an abundant harvest." And I have heard that there are several such things as auspicious grain, double water lilies, "rejoicing union" flowers, trees that grow together, and two heads of grain on one stalk. [But] produce on the same stalk I had never heard of or seen. So I greatly wondered at it.

Moreover, I come from a farming family. I personally tilled the ditch-drained fields. Yearly I saw the five grains grow and develop, but I never heard of sharing a stalk! I lived among the group of heroes for eleven years, and as king and as emperor have already recorded ten years. I have never heard of this good omen! Because I am not familiar with the *Odes* and *Documents*, I lack a broad view of antiquity and modern times. That must be why.

At the time when I was presented with the melons, the group of ministers took their virtue as redounding to me. When I listened to their speeches, I felt anxious and ashamed. I don't presume to call forth omens with my virtue but only pray for the harvest to be abundant and the people happy. I fundamentally am of slight virtue, but even if I had virtue, the Lord-on-high could not respond with a good omen to make me arrogant. If I committed a slight transgression, He would surely announce it with a bad sign to make me careful about my person, and to not let the people reach the point of calamity.

In antiquity and today, the auspicious signs of the five grains and the lucky omens of vegetation have roots nourished in rich soil. Any omens or blessings that come from the products of a piece of land not bigger than several feet or tens of inches or so must redound to the one who owns and manages it. It has nothing to do with me! Things like this, that grow and develop and bear fruit, and that are seen by people of the world—how can they be compared to things like the double pear, the fiery jujube, and the fairy peach, of which one hears, but which one cannot see? Whatever five-grains or vegetable lucky omens arise within a piece of land of several feet, several tens of inches, or several *mou*, they only congratulate him who owns and manages it!

If throughout the space between Heaven and Earth the times are peaceful and the harvest abundant, *that* is the sign of kingly rule. Kingly omens do not exist among trivialities! I kowtow in reverence to Heaven and sincerely respect Earth. So I chant verses in praise, saying:

> Heaven is a marvelous mirror;
> The gods of Earth match.
> They know that my good people
> work hard at farming from morning to night.
> Heaven's *qi* descends;
> Earth's *qi* rises up.
> The yellow springs and the fertile earth
> take shape together.
> From the same stalk double produce
> came from Jurong.
> The commoner did not eat it himself,
> but with sunburned back came to the court.
> Blue-green clouds of many colors,
> partly like emerald, partly like coral.

I split it and drink the juice:
crossing Chu, eating duckweed.
The commoner's heart is filial and obedient.
How could I have any ability?
Clumsily I utter a few phrases
to praise the sincerity of the commoner.
I wish you in every generation
a harmonious family and a peaceful home,
and determined sons and grandsons
[like] enfeoffed lords, [or] ranked dukes.
Be it for a thousand or ten thousand years,
do not forget to work at farming.

Major Dynastic Periods of Chinese History

Shang	商	c. 1600–1045 B.C.
Zhou	周	1045–256
Qin	秦	221–207
Han	漢	207 B.C.–220 A.D.
Jin	晉	317–419
Liu Song	劉宋	420–478
Sui	隋	581–617
Tang	唐	618–907
Song	宋	960–1276
Yuan	元	1234–1366
Ming	明	1368–1644
Qing	清	1644–1911

Reign Periods of the Ming Dynasty

Reign Title[1]	Reign Years	
Hongwu (*Hung-wu*)	1368–1398	Zhu Yuanzhang 朱元璋 Ming Taizu 明太祖
Jianwen (*Chien-wen*)	1399–1402	Son of Taizu's first son
Yongle (*Yung-lo*)	1402–1424	Zhu Di 朱棣 Taizong 明太宗 Fourth son of Taizu
Hongxi (*Hung-hsi*)	1425	
Xuande (*Hsüan-te*)	1426–1435	Ming Xuanzang
Zhengtong (*Cheng-t'ung*)	1435–1449	Zhu Qizhen
Jingtai (*Ching-t'ai*)	1450–1456	Brother of Qizhen
Tianshun (*T'ien-shun*)	1457–1464	Qizhen again
Chenghua (*Ch'eng-hua*)	1465–1487	
Hongzhi (*Hung-chih*)	1488–1505	
Zhengde (*Cheng-te*)	1506–1521	
Jiajing (*Chia-ching*)	1522–1566	First cousin of Zhengde
Longqing (*Lung-ch'ing*)	1567–1572	
Wanli (*Wan-li*)	1573–1619	
Taichang (*T'ai-ch'ang*)	1620	
Tianqi (*T'ien-ch'i*)	1621–1627	
Chongzhen (*Ch'ung-chen*)	1628–1644	

[1] There are two systems of Chinese romanization, *pinyin* and *Wade-Giles*. Pinyin is used throughout this book, but the Wade-Giles spellings of the reign periods are shown here in parentheses, as an additional point of reference.

Chronology of Main Events

1352 Zhu Yuanzhang joins a rebel religious group, the Red Turbans

1355 Zhu and his forces cross the Yangzi River

1356 Zhu consults with Cishan and seizes Nanjing

1367 Jurong presents auspicious grain to Zhu

1372 Audience in which Zhang Guan's melons are presented

1388 Temple to Cishan built at Nanjing

1389 Stele on Cishan requested by Jurong

c. 1391 Guan and Qian are executed; Yi and Da go into exile

1406 Zhang Jian is born

1439 Jian passes the *jinshi* examination

1443 Jian's mother dies, Jian begins three years' mourning

1452 Jian's parents and wives are honored by the Jingtai emperor

c. 1454 Yi returns to Jurong

c. 1456 Yi dies at age eighty-three; Jian begins three years' mourning

1471 Jian dies in office

1472 Prefect establishes Jian and Yi in shrine to local worthies

1492 Compilation of Jurong county gazetteer begins

1524 Portuguese eyewitness accounts of Ming China begin

The Zhang Family

Madam Hu 胡, wife of Zhang Guan

Madam Ni 倪, wife of Zhang Qian

Madam Sun 孫, wife of Guan's son Yi

Madam Tan 譚, wife of Guan's son Da

Madam Wang 王, Guan's grandmother, wife of Zhang Jinfu

Zhang Boqi 張伯啓, younger son of Guan, brother of Yi

Zhang Da 張達, Guan's eldest son, brother of Yi. Style name Boda 伯達

Zhang Guan 張觀, Jurong native who grew double melons. Style name Gubin 穀賓

Zhang Gushan 張穀善, brother of Guan and Qian. (This is his style name.)

Zhang Jian 張諫 (1406–1471), son of Yi, grandson of Guan. Style name Mengbi 孟弼

Zhang Jinfu 張進甫, grandfather of Guan

Zhang Mengzhao 張孟昭, son of Yi, grandson of Guan. (This is his style name.)

Zhang Qian 張謙, brother of Guan, unjustly accused. Style name Gugong 穀恭

Zhang Quanyi 張全一, sister of Guan

Zhang Shouzhen 張守貞, possibly a sister of Jinfu

Zhang Wencong 張文聰, father of Guan and Qian, grandfather of Yi

Zhang Yi 張遺, Guan's younger son. Style name Bo'an 伯安, called Yishan yilao 已山遺老

The Zhang Family Tree[*]

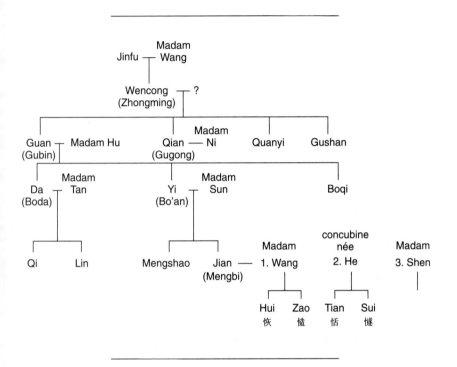

---

*This reconstructed family tree is incomplete, omitting many sons and all daughters except Quanyi.

Types of Documents

Collected works: When a literatus died, or sometimes before, his works would be edited and compiled by a son or student, and if the person was eminent enough or a good enough writer, the compilation would be printed and sold. Many of the other kinds of texts listed here were preserved in the collected works of the author, as were other public documents like prayers and judgments he had issued while in office, and what had originally been private or semi-private texts, like letters and poems.

Edict: an order or law issued by the emperor or in his name. The central state also issued documents such as commendations of virtuous persons, which might include instructions to local officials that such people be rewarded.

Epitaph: an account of a person's life, written at his or her death. There are different kinds. For officials, one would be drafted by a son or student to be submitted to the government. Another would be buried with the person's body, and another would be carved as a stele on his tomb. The family would ask eminent men with whom they had some kind of connection to write these texts, and the authors might be paid. Any epitaph might be preserved in the collected works of the writer or the subject, as well as in other compilations, such as collections of biographies.

Family instructions: A patriarch of a large family, or the head of a clan or lineage organization, might write out family instructions that his descendants were supposed to follow, but which were not legally binding. Sometimes such instructions were published for the edification of the greater public. Taizu's "August Ming Ancestral Instruction" was family instructions for his descendants and was supposed to be binding on them.

Fiction: In the late Ming period, short stories and novels that were made up just for entertainment value were very popular, as were plays. Fiction in China developed out of oral traditions of story telling and out of Buddhist religious tales. Historians use fiction carefully as a source for understandings of and assumptions about daily life that the authors apparently shared with their readers.

Folk tales: Plenty of stories about gods and men were told that were not written down. But literati collected some oral traditions and wrote them down. Later story tellers might re-tell written stories, so there was a constant process of give and take between the oral and written media.

Gazetteer: also called "local history." A gazetteer focuses on a particular geographical unit, from empire on down to district, or a particular institution, such as a temple. It includes all kinds of information from different periods and by different authors. County gazetteers, such as those for Jurong, include geographical and administrative information, such as rough maps and tax and population figures for each district; lists and biographies of local people honored in various categories, such as those who have passed each level of examination, donors to charity, chaste widows, and filial sons; lists and biographies of officials who have served there; histories of the various local institutions, including temples, schools, and offices; records of antiquities, notable graves, scenic spots (sometimes with pictures), historical events, and strange stories; poems and other writings by men of the place or by visitors to it; and all kinds of other things. Each gazetteer is a little different, in part because compilers had their own agendas. Every sixty years or so (very roughly) a county would issue a new version of its gazetteer, and the new compilers usually included much of the information in the previous one.

Genealogy: a compilation of documents about a clan or lineage, usually including a family tree going back as many generations as were known. As new editions were re-issued, the old prefaces, often by men from outside the clan, were not thrown out, but incorporated as points of pride and history in themselves. Women were often omitted from the family tree.

Histories: The official history of each dynasty was compiled under the dynasty that followed it. The *Mingshi* (Official history of the Ming dynasty) was issued by the Qing dynasty in 1736 after a long and contentious process that earlier had drawn in many scholars who had worked under the Ming dynasty. In addition to these official dynastic histories, there were private histories of the dynasty, of particular institutions, and so on.

Laws: The word of the emperor was law, but there was a written legal code, the *Great Ming Code*, which was revised from time to time and to which magistrates and prefects, who were responsible for settling lawsuits and punishing criminals, could refer.

Memorial: a report, suggestion, criticism, or other communication from an official to an emperor.

Ode: a poem written in praise of something or someone.

Poems: Writing poems was an essential social and literary skill, as much as a means of personal expression. Some poems, like the ancient ones in the *Book of Songs*, were meant to be sung. People memorized reams of poetry, and some famous poems were well known even to the illiterate. Lines and images from well-known poems entered everyday language. Poetry was an area in which women writers published very successfully in the Ming period.

Postface: a short essay commenting on another work, placed at the end.

Preface: a short essay introducing another work, placed at the beginning.

Proclamation: a text from the government read and announced to the public.

Record, or commemorative inscription: When a school or other institution was built or rebuilt, or when there were other events worth commemorating, those involved would ask a literary man to write a record that described what had been done and by whom, and why it was important. Often the record was inscribed as a stele and put up at the place in question, as well as copied into the local gazetteer and the collected works of the man who wrote it.

Regulations: Villages and lineages or clans sometimes had their own regulations.

Stele, or inscription: Any kind of text could be made into a stele, that is, engraved on stone and set up in a public place. It might stand on the back of a stone turtle or be embedded into a plaster wall.

Veritable Records: a day-by-day account of the important events and imperial actions of one reign, compiled in the next reign from court diaries and other documents.

Notes

Introduction (see pp. xi–xxiii)

1. *Tang liudian* 唐六典, in Twitchett, *The Writing of Official History*, 13.

2. Twitchett, *The Writing of Official History*, 13, 27–29, 10.

3. For details on Zhu's vision for China, see Farmer, *Zhu Yuanzhang and Early Ming Legislation*.

4. Campany, *Strange Writing*, 8–14.

5. Nicholson, *God's Secretaries*, 140–41.

6. For vivid portraits of late Ming China, see among other books Brook, *Confusions of Pleasure*, and Cass, *Dangerous Women*.

7. Yang, *Ming Da Gao yanjiu*, 153.

8. Zhu Yuanzhang, *Da Gao* (translated as *Great Warning, Grand Pronouncement, Great Announcements*, etc.) 2.52, in Dardess, *Confucianism and Autocracy*, 245–46.

9. Zhu Yuanzhang, "The August Ming Ancestral Instruction" (*Huang Ming zu xun* 皇明祖訓), in Farmer, *Zhu Yuanzhang and Early Ming Legislation*, 121. Farmer here also translates many other documents by the Ming founder.

10. Zhu Yuanzhang, "The August Ming Ancestral Instruction," in Farmer, *Zhu Yuanzhang and Early Ming Legislation*, 122–24.

11. *Han shu* 漢書 56/4, in Lippiello, *Auspicious Omens and Miracles*, 247.

12. In Thompson, *The Chinese Way in Religion*, 179–80.

13. Erik Zürcher, "Forward," in Lippiello, *Auspicious Omens and Miracles*.

14. Kuan Han-ch'ing (c. 1241–c. 1322), "The Injustice Done to Tou Ngo," in Liu, *Six Yuan Plays*.

15. Eberhard, "The Political Function of Astronomy and Astronomers in Han China," 41, 52–53, 69. Eberhard uses astrological practice to assess Chinese despotism. He makes the following points with regard to portents, or ill omens (for there are few good omens in the Han records he studies): (a) natural anomalies were believed to be connected with bad happenings; (b) historians sometimes explained a portent differently from the way it was explained when it happened; (c) historians and theorists used various methods of interpretation and often explained the same portent differently; (d) portents could be taken to refer to members of the court other than the emperor and could result in physical punishments for them; (e) portents could be interpreted by one faction at court to the detriment of another; and (f) given this, and given that portents were sometimes fabricated (five out of twelve eclipses were invented, he finds), there were surely some people who did not believe in them at all.

16. Elvin, "Female Virtue and the State in China," 116.

17. Feng Menglong, "Monk Moon Bright Redeems Willow Green," translated in Yang and Yang, *Stories Old and New*, 512.

18. Lederose, *Ten Thousand Things*, 177.

19. See Brokaw, *Ledgers of Merit and Demerit*.

20. Feng, "Old Man Zhang Grows Melons and Marries Wennü" 張古老種瓜聚文女, translated in Yang and Yang, *Stories Old and New*, 575–76.

21. de Rada, *Relation of the Things of China*.

22. Campany, *Strange Writing*, 190, 305–6, 351–57.

23. Chan, "The Rise of Ming T'ai-tsu (1368–1398)," 708.

24. Zürcher, Erik "Forward," in Lipiello, *Auspicious Omens and Miracles*.

25. See plates 29, 30, and 32 in Laing, *Art and Aesthetics in Chinese Popular Prints*.

Chapter I (see pp. 1–13)

1. Two books open with engaging, detailed descriptions of the Ming emperors' daily life, so I will not duplicate their efforts. For the early

Ming, see Tsai, *Perpetual Happiness: The Ming Emperor Yongle*; for the late Ming, see Huang, *1587: A Year of No Significance*.

2. *Li ji* (*Record of Rites*), book one, I, 3, p. 82, cited in Thompson, *Chinese Religion*, 39, prescribes: "He who pares a melon for the Son of Heaven should divide it into four parts and then into eight, and cover them with a napkin of fine linen. For the ruler of a state, he should divide it into four parts and cover them with a coarse napkin. To a great officer, he should [present the four parts] uncovered. An inferior officer should receive it [simply] with the stalk cut away. A common man will deal with it with his teeth."

3. Zhu Yuanzhang (Ming Taizu), "In Praise of Auspicious Melons" (Jia gua zan). The preface, also called the essay, has 454 characters, and the ode 100 characters. This and other translations are my own unless otherwise specified. See Appendix for translation. For a discussion of Taizu's melon ode, his order that Song Lian write one, and his influence on local literature, see Rao, "Mingchu shiwen de zouxiang," 46.

4. For Xie's authorship of the *Ming Taizu shilu*, see Chan, "Xie Jin (1369–1415) as an Imperial Propagandist."

5. The *Veritable Records* version of the audience, in 224 characters, without any ode or mention of an ode, is found at *Ming Taizu shilu* 4/74/1370. Xie Jin must have had a draft court account to work with, because he mentions one fact that does not appear in either Taizu's or Song Lian's account. Since historiographical duties were assigned to the Hanlin Academy, the official court account may also have been written by Song, who requested that one be made, or it may have been part of the *Da Ming rili* (Daily Records of the Great Ming) compiled the next year (see Franke, "Historical Writing during the Ming," 741).

6. For a summary of the structure of Ming government, see Hucker, *A Dictionary of Official Titles in Imperial China*, 70–82.

7. On Taizu's plans for state and society, see Farmer, *Zhu Yuanzhang and Early Ming Legislation*.

8. Twitchett, *The Writing of Official History*, 86.

9. Dardess, *Confucianism and Autocracy*, 170.

10. Song Lian, "Hymn on Auspicious Melons" (Jia gua song 嘉瓜頌). There is a preface of about 525 characters and an ode of about 224 characters. In (*Huang*) *Ming Wenheng* 19/8–9 in the *Siku quanshu* electronic edition.) Shen Yue, "Furui zhi" 符瑞志 (Treatise on Omens), in *Song shu* 3/29/833–34. Shen's descriptions of the melons include the terms *jia gua* 嘉瓜 (auspicious melons), *tongdi* 同蒂 (sharing a stem), and *yi ti* 異體 (anomalous in form).

11. Han Yu, "Zou Bianzhou de jiamu jiagua zhuang" 奏汴州得嘉禾嘉瓜壯, in *Han Changli wenji jiaozhu*, 426.

12. Song Lian, "Hymn on Auspicious Melons."

13. Song Lian, "Hymn on Auspicious Melons."

14. On omens as propaganda in the Han period see Wu, *The Wu Liang Shrine*, 96. On flattering emperors by saying that they had accomplished the Great Peace (*Tai Ping*), see Loewe, "The Cycle of Cathay," 314.

15. Chan, "The Rise of Ming T'ai-tsu," 709. For translations of accounts of miracles in Taizu's life, as well as consideration of their relationship to the *Veritable Records*, see also Chan, "Xie Jin as Imperial Propagandist," 86–121.

16. Goodrich and Fang, *Dictionary of Ming Biography*, 1391. On Han encouragement, see Wu, *The Wu Liang Shrine*, 96.

17. On the identities and fates of these officials, see Goodrich and Fang, *Dictionary of Ming Biography*, 639–640, 853, 1228–29, 1389–92; Dreyer, *Early Ming China*, 98–100; Franke, "Historical Writing during the Ming," 778; and Zhang Tingyu, *Mingshi* 10/105 (itself a vivid testimony to Taizu's vicious destruction of trusted advisers— the first generation of most noble lines is the only one recorded, followed by pages of blank lines where successor generations should be), 11/199, 12/127/3773–74, 26/380/7908.

18. Memorial of 1388, in Langlois, "The Hung-wu Reign," 156.

19. The term first described how the Yongle emperor persecuted every family member and every person from the native village of a man who had tried to kill him and spat blood on him before being executed. "Melon-vine guilt" evokes both the tenuousness of the victims' connections with the traitor and the way the persecution

rapidly spread in every direction. Goodrich and Fang, *Dictionary of Ming Biography*, 249.

20. *Ming Taizu shilu* 4/74/1370.

21. Li, *Ming Taizu*, 1–2.

22. See for instance Liu, *Guochu shiji*, 629 (19b): "Taizu once said: 'Haozhou [i.e., Fengyang] is my family's native place (*wu jia xiang* 吾家鄉).'"

23. Farmer, *Early Ming Government*, 48–53.

24. da Cruz, "Treatise in Which the Things of China Are Related at Great Length . . . ," 56.

25. Song Lian, "Hymn on Auspicious Melons."

26. Cleaves, "The Memorial for Presenting the *Yuan Shih*," 64. Cleaves interprets *gua fen* 瓜 分 as referring to a melon left to dry out in the field after the harvest, but it simply refers to the ease with which melons are sliced up for serving, particularly those that are striped, ribbed, or fissured into segments. This metaphor for partition of the national territory was revived to describe the "scramble for concessions" by Japan and the West after 1895. Foreign powers encroached and made demands even after the fall of the Qing dynasty and the establishment of the Republic of China in 1912. In 1934, Japan occupied Manchuria in Northeast China. Many intellectuals felt frustrated by what they perceived as their countrymen's unconcern with national humiliation. One writer, whose anthologist described him as a rural medieval Buddhist reborn into the twentieth century, wrote a satirical essay entitled "Eating Melon Seeds." Young men can do it with a cigarette in one hand, their teeth making a "crack, plop" sound, he explained; young women manage to make even the spitting out of the shell alluring. The perfect way to kill time, this skill was the special genius of Chinese people—the Japanese people could not manage it properly. "After racking my brains to think of foodstuffs which fully meet the above requirements for killing time, there is only one in the world I can come up with, and that is melon seeds. That is why I said the person who discovered them was a veritable genius. And the Chinese, who enjoy melon seeds to the full, are truly wonderful exponents of the profession of killing time. Consider the roaring trade done by

confectionary shops and southern food shops, consider the melon seed husks that cover the floors of teashops, wineshops and homes, and it is obvious that the amount of time killed amid the sound of 'crack, plop' and 'dik-dik' in the course of a year is staggering. If in future this profession expands further, I fear that the whole of China will go to extinction amid the sounds of 'crack, plop' and 'dik-dik.'" Feng, "Eating Melon Seeds," 195. In the Republic, it was not the ruler alone who bore the responsibility for disaster, but the people as a whole.

27 Song Lian, "Hymn on Auspicious Melons."

28. Langlois, "The Hung-wu Reign," 100, 103, 129. Rossabi, "Ming Foreign Policy: The Case of Hami," 83. Melons had long been grown in China proper, however. The types of melons grown in Huzhou, not far from Nanjing and Jurong, were catalogued in a local gazetteer from the early thirteenth century. The author commented that some could be eaten raw, so they were probably similar to the melons presented to Taizu. 1201–4 *Jiatai Wuxing Zhi.*

29. Farmer, *Zhu Yuanzhang and Early Ming Legislation,* 47.

30. Zhu Yuanzhang, "The August Ming Ancestral Instruction," in Farmer, *Zhu Yuanzhang and Early Ming Legislation,* 121.

31. de Crespigny, *Portents of Protest in the Later Han Dynasty,* 15. See also Wu, *The Wu Liang Shrine,* 94–103.

32. Cheng, "What Did It Mean to be a *Ru* in Han Times?" 110. Wu, *The Wu Liang Shrine,* 96, 102.

33. Zhu Yuanzhang, "The August Ming Ancestral Instruction," in Farmer, *Zhu Yuanzhang and Early Ming Legislation,* 121. Eberhard, "The Political Function of Astronomy," 50, 53, concludes that five out of twelve Han eclipses were fabricated, mainly by officials and historians to criticize the emperor or attack a rival faction at court.

Chapter II (see pp. 14–26)

1. Song Lian, "Hymn on Auspicious Melons."

2. Wu, *The Wu Liang Shrine,* 94.

3. Eberhard, "The Political Function of Astronomy and Astronomers in Han China," 47.

4. I think we can reasonably accept, for the sake of argument, that much of what Taizu wrote in his essay he had earlier actually said to the assembled ministers. The *Veritable Records* compilers could have retroactively put his written words into the conversation. But Song Lian also reports portions of what he said, and I believe that his piece was written very shortly after the original discussion, probably before he had seen Taizu's own piece, and perhaps before the latter had been written.

5. "Monthly Ordinances" section of *Li ji* (the *Record of Rites*), 255.

6. For the examination system, see Miyazaki, *China's Examination Hell*, and Elman, *A Cultural History of Civil Examinations*.

7. Zhu Yuanzhang, "In Praise of Auspicious Melons."

8. In Farmer, *Zhu Yuanzhang and Early Ming Legislation*, 43. Taizu attributes these words to a visitor.

9. Zhu Yuanzhang, "In Praise of Auspicious Melons."

10. Ibid.

11. For a fascinating discussion of the Qing emperors' sense of this direct communication and of their explanations of moral responsibility for good and bad weather, see Elvin, "Who Was Responsible for the Weather?"

12. Langlois, "The Hung-wu Reign," 108.

13. Ho, "Ideological Implications of Major Sacrifices in Early Ming," 61–62.

14. *Ming Taizu Shilu* 4/74/1370.

15. Xie reports a similar modesty with regard to omens on Taizu's part in "Ming di dian ti ci" 明帝典題詞, in his *Wenyi ji* 16/3a.

16. *Ming Taizu Shilu* 4/74/1370.

17. Eberhard, "The Political Function of Astronomy and Astronomers in Han China," 54.

18. Zhu Yuanzhang, "In Praise of Auspicious Melons."

19. Campany, *Strange Writing*, 335.

20. Zhu Yuanzhang, "In Praise of Auspicious Melons."

21. Only the *Veritable Records* report this, showing that Xie Jin must have had a separate contemporary account to work with.

22. For the phases of construction of local order in the Hongwu reign, see Schneewind, "Visions and Revisions."

23. Xie, *Wenyi ji*, 3a; Chan, "The Rise of Ming T'ai-tsu," 708–9.

24. Translated in Chan, "Xie Jin as Imperial Propagandist," 85.

25. Peter Ditmanson, personal communication, 2004.

26. Dardess, *Confucianism and Autocracy*, 263–64. Franke writes that "chances for the author [of a portion of the *Veritable Records*] to express his personal opinion rested mainly in the selection of some documents and the suppression of others. In this way, fact and events could be greatly misrepresented. In addition, documents could be condensed so as deliberately to distort the original meaning" ("Historical Writing during the Ming," 747).

27. Chan, "Xie Jin as Imperial Propagandist," 81.

28. Campany, *Strange Writing*, 13.

Chapter III (see pp. 27–36)

1. The provincial divisions were somewhat unstable; see Hucker, "Ming Government," 11–14. On Nanzhili, see Heijdra, "The Socio-Economic Development of Ming Rural China," 57. On Jurong, see 1994 *Jurong xianzhi*, 128.

2. The version I used of Song Lian's hymn and preface does not even report the prefect's surname, but the Wanli prefectural gazetteer I gleaned the surname from, which lists Zhang Yulin as prefect from 1372 to 1374 (and again in the Jianwen period), says that its source for that listing is "Hymn on Auspicious Melons" (1577 *Yingtian fuzhi* 6/1–2). A native of Luzhou 廬州, Zhang Yulin had earlier served the Ming dynasty as subprefect of Taizhou 泰州, according to the 1810/1817 *Chongxiu Yangzhou fuzhi* 37/52a.

3. Sun, *Zhu Yuanzhang xinian yaolu*, 225.

4. Campany, *Strange Writing*, 8–14.

5. See Jiang, *The Great Ming Code*, Article 105, "Eating Melons or Fruits of Gardens or Orchards without Authorization." Locally, an 1808 stele records an agreement of ten villages to prohibit activities like letting one's cattle eat other people's grain, sleeping or eating in temples, stealing grain from the fields or fish from the ponds, and so on. The sixth article stipulates a penalty of 2 taels of silver for stealing melons, fruit, vegetables or plants. The stele is in the Jurong county museum, in the reconstructed Huayang Academy in Immortal Ge (Hong) Public Park.

6. Loewe, "China," 39.

7. Strickmann, "The Maoshan Revelations," 60.

8. The eastern *gua* is also beneficial. The perfectly white *gua* of Yue and the cucumber and summer squash (yellow *gua*) have no special power, apparently. Wang, *San tsai tuhui*, 2506.

9. Chan, "Xie Jin as Imperial Propagandist," 90.

10. Langlois, "The Hung-wu Reign," 174; Chan, "The Chien-wen, Yung-lo, Hung-hsi, and Hsüan-te Reigns, 1399–1435," 272.

11. 1750/1900 *Jurong xianzhi*, 89–90, 93. The gazetteer comments that these many products attest to the preciousness of the soil. The magic fungus was a popular symbol, often made into a wooden or jade scepter called a *ruyi* 如意 or "as you wish." Such scepters can be seen in many museum collections and are depicted in paintings and prints.

12. In the Ming period, auspicious melons appeared in other places too. The 1735 *Shaanxi tongzhi* (47/69) notes that according to the biographical collection *Ming shan cang*, in August–September 1432, auspicious grain and auspicious melons both appeared in Shaanxi. The 1741 *Guizhou tongzhi* j. 37 records a "Hymn to Auspicious Melons" (Jiagua song 嘉瓜頌) by Wang Xun 王訓 about some melons that appeared in Guizhou. The text straightforwardly praises the Ming, both emperors and ministers, for their benevolent rule bringing great peace to the ten thousand directions, and the text makes everything, even the weather that produced the melons, depend on the emperor's virtue.

13. Zhu Yuanzhang, "Yu Jurong xian min ling" 諭句容縣民令, in Qian, *Quan Ming wen* 1/300.

14. 1750/1900 *Jurong xianzhi*, 1301 (last j./9).

15. Wang Zhi (1379–1462), in Dardess, *A Ming Society*, 38.

16. 1496 *Jurong xianzhi*, 405 (6/3); 1750/1900 *Jurong xianzhi*, 617 (7/30a); 1904 *Xucuan Jurong xianzhi* 18middle/47a. 1750/1900 *Jurong xianzhi* 617 (7/30a) says that the stele is inside the Mingde hall of the school. See Lippiello, *Auspicious Omens*, chapter 2, on the natural world reflecting the virtue of resident administrators.

17. 1496 *Jurong xianzhi*, 466ff., (6/20–25). For Wang Shao see 419 (6/32), for the magistrates' names and dates see 366 (3/4), for their biographies see 406 (6/5–7), but the activities of the magistrates are evident throughout the gazetteer. Another poem commemorates Magistrate Wang's successful prayers for rain. For Xu Guang see 1750/1900 *Jurong xianzhi*, 490ff. (6/6ff.)

18. Yang Shiyuan reprinted only the text, not the pictures, but laid out the page to indicate where on the inscription each picture appeared: the bamboo in the upper right, the melons lower and to the left, the grain further left and a bit higher. He also gave the dimensions of the stele and its characters. Yang, *Jurong jinshi ji* 5/18–19.

19. 1904 *Xucuan Jurong xianzhi* 18middle/47a.

20. Laing, *Art and Aesthetics in Chinese Popular Prints*, 84–85.

21. Ni, "Yishan xiansheng Zhang gong ai ci, bing xu".

22. Liu Song (1321–1381), in Dardess, *A Ming Society*, 17.

23. Among the Jurong men who gained office through recommendation was one surnamed Zhang. 1750/1900 *Jurong xianzhi* 8/22 (652). The expression "*tou gua bao yu*" 投瓜報玉 comes from the *Book of Songs* (Airs of the States, 64), where it refers to lovers exchanging flowering quince for jade ornaments. It came to mean getting something valuable in return for something small.

24. Yang, *Jurong jinshi ji*, 7/1–2 gives the text of the "Yuzhi jia gua gong," namely Zhu Yuanzhang's "In Praise of Auspicious Melons," dated Hongwu 5.6.28, appending the text from the *Wulun shu*, copied from the gazetteer (see Chapter VI). The presentation of the ode in the 1496 *Jurong xianzhi* (7/4b) among other imperial edicts also suggests that it was engraved. The 1904 gazetteer lists it but does not note that it still exists, although 59 of the 130 Ming inscriptions listed are noted as still existing.

Chapter IV (see pp. 37–57)

1. Dardess, *Confucianism and Autocracy*, 259.

2. 1496 *Jurong xianzhi* 6/51 (430). Zhang Yi died at eighty-three in 1453–1454 and had been in his late teens when his uncle and father were executed, placing that incident at around 1390. The "Righteous Mound" was 3 *li* south of the county seat, near the South Bridge: 張觀墓在縣南三里許南橋義壟 (1676 *Jurong xianzhi* 2/40–41 [73–74]).

3. Zhang Jian's four sons Hui, Zao, Tian, and Sui, for instance, each had a heart radical in his one-character name, as did Zhang Hui and Zhang Cong, minor degree holders of 1470 and 1472 (1496 *Jurong xianzhi* 6/37, 6/40). Zhang Heng was made an honorary official with cap and belt for donating grain, as were two Zhang brothers named Mengchun and Mengfu (1496 *Jurong xianzhi* 6/59–60); they may have been of the same generation as Jian and his elder brother, styled Mengbi and Mengzhao, respectively.

4. In Ho, "Plant Symbolism in the Religious Poems of the *Book of Poetry*," 166.

5. Anonymous, Han period, "Gu er xing" 孤兒行, in Jiang, *Mianmian si yuan dao*, 93ff.

6. Family division was forbidden until the parents had died, but the law was not always followed; see Article 93, "Establishing Separate Household Registration," of Jiang, *The Great Ming Code*. On division, see Wakefield, *Household Division and Inheritance in Qing and Republican China*. On honors, see Elvin, "Female Virtue and the State in China," 126.

7. Translated in Chan, "Xie Jin as Propagandist," 87.

8. *Zhang jia zupu*, 29ff.

9. According to Ming law, the wives and concubines of an offender sent into life exile were required to follow him, but his father, paternal grandfather, sons, and sons' sons were only permitted to do so, if they wished. *The Great Ming Code* (Article 15) does not comment on brothers accompanying exiles. See Jiang, *The Great Ming Code*.

10. Bray, *Technology and Gender*, part 3, shows that under some circumstances it might in fact be the duty of a gentry wife to abort a fetus. Bray also discusses gender separation, including matters of work and status, and the physical and ideological layout of the home.

11. The women's biographies appear in the 1900 reprint of the 1750 *Jurong xianzhi* 842–43 (9/2–3). Zhang Jian's biography of a chaste widow, Madame Wang, appears on p. 847. The 1496 *Jurong xianzhi* has the same biographies, except for Madame Tan's, with a few very minor differences, see 432–33 (6/54ff.).

12. Ni, "Yishan xiansheng Zhang gong ai ci, bing xu."

13. 1496 *Jurong xianzhi* 6/51 (430). This was in the early Ming period, as one member of the next generation earned his metropolitan degree under the Yongle emperor.

14. Smedley, *The Great Road*, 15–17.

15. Smedley, *The Great Road*, 9, 12.

16. *Mingshi* 24/282/7223, biography of Fan Zugan 范祖幹. Fan nurtured his parents so that they both lived to be over eighty, even though he was too poor to bury them properly when they died and he had to get help from neighbors.

17. Nivison, "Aspects of Traditional Chinese Biography," 463.

18. Shang Lu, "Taipu Zhang gong shendao bei."

19. Ni, "Yishan xiansheng Zhang gong ai ci, bing xu."

20. 1750/1900 *Jurong xianzhi*, 792 (9/46b).

21. Shang, "Taipu Zhang gong shendao bei."

22. 1750/1900 *Jurong xianzhi*, 82 (1/17b).

23. 1604 *Laizhou fuzhi* 2/7. Zhang Jian served in Laizhou from about 1468 to 1471 (Guo, *Benchao fensheng renwu kao* 30/115/3 (10101–2; but see below). *Ming Xianxong shilu* 43/91/1764, for Chenghua 7, fifth moon. Jian's promotions were separately recorded in the *Veritable Records* as well of course, for instance *Ming Yingzong shilu* 30/175/3386.

24. Zhu Yuanzhang, *Da Gao* 1.24, in Dardess, *Confucianism and Autocracy*, 231.

25. Zhu Yuanzhang, *Da Gao* 2.7, in Dardess, *Confucianism and Autocracy*, 234.

26. da Cruz, "Treatise in Which the Things of China Are Related at Great Length . . . ," 147–48.

27. Chan, "Xie Jin as Imperial Propagandist," 77.

28. See Huang, *1587: A Year of No Significance*, 21ff.

29. See Kutcher, *Mourning in Late Imperial China*.

30. Chen Tian 陳田, *Ming shi jishi* 明詩記事, vol. 3, 705 (64/17/5). Zhang Jian's son Hui was granted the title of judge (*tongban*) of Huangzhou in Huguang because of Jian's merit (1750/1900 *Jurong xianzhi* 8/25). Such auspicious signs were not unique to Zhang Jian. A few years after Zhang Jian died, a member of the Ming royal family earned by his filiality in residing at his father's grave various signs, including a pair of auspicious melons, two on one stalk (Xi'an shi wenwu baohu kaogu suo, "Xi'an nanjiao huang Ming zongshi Qianyang Duanyi wang Zhu gong Zeng mu qingli jianbao," 44). See also *Ming Xiaozong shilu* j. 181, for Hongzhi 14, eleventh month, *renwu* day. One source notes that the term *rui niao* (auspicious birds) could refer to meritorious officials, which makes them a particularly appropriate sign of approval for Zhang Jian (Zhu, *Wang Yangming zai Qian shiwen zhuyi*, 20).

31. Wan Sitong, *Mingshi chaoben* 392/15b, section on filiality.

32. Shang, "Taipu Zhang gong shendao bei."

33. See Xu, *Xu Wei ji* (reprint, Beijing: Zhonghua shuju, 1983), 410. Kathleen Ryor, personal communication, February 17, 2006.

34. 1555 *Guizhou tongzhi* 9/37 (348). Zhang Bo'an (Zhang Yi) is the first person listed under Chishui guard for "our dynasty's local men." The biography says: "A man of the guard. He studied, loved propriety, and was especially honored for his filial piety and brotherly harmony, purity, and frugality. Later he was given the honorary title of investigating censor because of his son. Zhang Jian: He was Bo'an's son. He was rich in literary learning and had the thoughts of a hero. . . . Known for his honesty. In office as investigating censor, his style was stern and harsh."

35. Chen, *Ming shi ji shi*, vol. 3, 705 (64/17/5). Chen introduces Zhang Jian as "the descendant of the Zhang Guan who presented auspicious melons in the Hongwu period."

36. Guo, *Benchao fensheng renwu kao* 4/12/27 (1073–74), 30/115/3 (10101–2). The two entries use slightly different versions of the character for "Jian" but give the same style name. This was probably also Wan Sitong's source on Zhang Jian. He Chuguang's compilation of brief career summaries of censors, *Lantai fa jian lu* (1597), also lists Jian as a Guizhou Chishui man and says nothing at all about his family.

37. Chen, *Ming shi ji shi*, vol. 3, 705(64/17/5).

38. Zhang Jian is listed as a Jurong native, but of a military registration, in the *Ming Qing jinshi timing beilu suoyin*, and his death notice in the *Ming Xianzong shilu* (43/91/1764) makes him a Jurong native.

39. The short biography of Zhang Jian "Daipu siqing Zhang gong Jian zhuan" 太僕寺卿張公諫傳 by Chen Gao 陳鎬 reports that "In early Hongwu, a garden produced auspicious melons. Grandfather Gubin presented them." Mentioning the texts by Ming Taizu and Song Lian, it continues: "a short time afterward, because his younger brother Gugong committed an offense [*de zui*], the family was exiled." Chen does not care whether the accusation was false, as the Jurong gazetteer insists, nor that the executions came some two decades after the presentation of the melons (Jiao, *Guochao xianzheng lu* 5/72/5). The *Shilu* biography of Jian, which Jiao also includes, mentions the exile but omits the melons.

40. 1496 *Jurong xianzhi*, 398 (5/26) lists Zhang Yi and Zhang Jian. There are twice-yearly ceremonies for the whole group. In Chenghua 7 (January 23, 1472), the prefect of Yingtian was ordered to arrange worship for Jian (1496 *Jurong xianzhi*, 456 [7/34]). Worship for Zhang Yi probably began at the same time.

41. Shang Lu's epitaph for Zhang Jian explicitly says: "His several sons are taking his coffin south and returning and are planning this year in the winter, twelfth month [January 27, 1472], to bury him south of the city in Fuxiang district at the Righteous Mound." Ni Qian's funerary verse for Zhang Yi refers to burial there. The list of tombs in the 1676 *Jurong xianzhi* 2/40–41 (73–74) records the burial

places of Zhang Guan and his brother and of Zhang Jian separately but identifies them both as being south of the county seat, at the Righteous Mound.

42. Before the Song dynasty, the temple had been in a place subsequently divined not to be good, and through the faults of previous magistrates there had been no school at all, resulting in "bad customs." Yang, *Jurong jinshi ji*, 4/6.

43. See 1750/1900 *Jurong xianzhi*, 270; 1496 *Jurong xianzhi*, 387 (5/4b) on the Righteous Platform; 398 (5/26) for his place in the shrine to local worthies; 427 (6/48b) for his biography; and other places. There is also a Song-era filial son named Zhang Xiaoyou 張孝友 who has a recorded tomb and appears in the gazetteer several times, but he is from north of the county seat, in Yifeng district. Zhang Changwei is recorded in the *(Da) Ming yitong zhi* 6/42b; in 1534 *Nanji zhi* 316; and in 1577 *Yingtian fuzhi* 30/8a, 21/45b.

44. See Yang, *Jurong jinshi ji* 8/10, 8/21–22, 1/2. Yang Shiyuan records a number of Tang and Song steles for Zhang Changwei, but there was a hiatus in the first half of the Ming period, until Wang Shen "noticed some broken-up traces of an eminent local man in an empty lot" and contacted eminent Jurong man Wang Wei to ask him about it.

45. *Yitai Zhang shi jiasheng* (Genealogy of the Yitai Zhang), 35–36, 95, 130. The first use of the term "Yitai" in prefaces to the Zhang genealogy is a reference to the street named after it. In 1409, a clan member wrote a preface to a new compilation he made of the genealogy. He explains with great emotion that his late father had been adopted out by his father into the Zhu 朱 family of Yitai Street. It was common for men or their widows without a son to adopt a child to carry on the man's line and offer ancestral worship, although in law and in Confucian ideology the child was supposed to be of the same surname, and preferably a nephew. The writer's father, on the orders of his father, had changed his surname and lived on Yitai Street with the Zhus. His son, the writer, knew nothing of this until one day his father led him by the hand to Daiting village east of the county seat and said, "This is my home of generations." Although legally and morally he was now a Zhu, his filial heart had never stopped thinking of Daiting, and he charged his son to remember this. The son apparently deserted the adoptive lineage. He made

sacrifices to his father in the Zhang ancestral temple and developed a burning interest in genealogy. Imagine his delight when one day a Zhang uncle found an old genealogical record hidden among the tiles of a deserted room! In this first reference, the Yitai was a place of exile, not a home.

46. See Yang, *Jurong jinshi ji*, 8/10, 8/21–22, 1/2.

Chapter V (see pp. 58–69)

1. Zhang, *Guoshi jiwen* 1/1: "The ancestors of [Taizu] were Jurong people." The early Ming "Zhu shi shi de beiji" begins by acknowledging the Jurong origins of the family. The district was called Tongde (Thorough Virtue) because a Song paragon had morally transformed all the inhabitants. During the Great Leap Forward, it became Stone Lion commune. The two impressive guardians of a princely tomb of the Liang dynasty narrowly escaped being dynamited by Red Guards during the Cultural Revolution. Local farmers stepped in to protect the lions after holes had already been drilled in the base of the male.

2. 1496 *Jurong xianzhi* 4/9b.

3. 1750/1900 *Jurong xianzhi* 61–62 (1/7), 196 (3/18).

4. Jurong difangzhi bangongshe, *Jurong minjian gushi*, 50–51.

5. Li, *Ming Taizu*, 1–2.

6. "Zhushi shide beiji," in Chan, "Xie Jin as Propagandist," 89.

7. Lu, *Shuyuan zaji* 3/26. Lu heard this from a native of Fengyang.

8. Taizu's descendants were no more interested in Jurong, despite at least one approach from the local side. In 1532, Jurong native Wang Wei—the same man to whom Magistrate Wang Shen turned at about the same time to revive the Yitai site after finding its traces—memorialized for a special tomb temple on the site, and the Jiajing emperor ordered some officials to investigate. They reported on the dragon-claw tree, a few Zhu family steles, and some modest graves, and they said that the place was now a field of about five *mou*

farmed by one Mr. Yang. The Jiajing emperor was unimpressed and the matter came to nought. Zhu, *Yongchuang xiaopin*, 6/1–2 (119); Tan, *Zaolin zazu* 東林雜俎 1/1.

9. For the influence on Taizu of his maternal grandfather, who was a fortune-teller and had fought against the Yuan invasion of the South, see Mote, "The Rise of the Ming Dynasty," 44.

10. Nanjing Xiaoling Bowuguan, *Ming Xiaoling zhi xinbian*, 219.

11. Xiaoling Museum of Nanjing, *Xiaoling Tomb of the Ming Dynasty*, 79.

12. Tan, "Xiaoling ye ku" 孝陵夜哭 (Crying in the night at the Filial Tomb), in his *Zaolin zazu*.

13. Stele from 1586–1587, copied into 1881 *Guangde zhouzhi* 13/14b. The Wanli-era Jurong gazetteer compilers noted Taizu's similar reaction to the landscape of Jurong, citing a stele by the Yongle emperor that described how his father was impressed with the auspicious nature of the Jurong scene with its high mountains and deep streams (preface to the Wanli edition of the gazetteer, copied into 1750/1900 *Jurong xianzhi*, 13 (old prefaces/1).

14. 1750/1900 *Jurong xianzhi*, 1157–60 (10/30–32). For a translation of Taizu's own account of a dream in which he asked another deity for reassurance and guidance, see Taylor, "Ming T'ai-tsu's Story of a Dream," and Chan, "Xie Jin as Propagandist," 100–2.

15. Zhou and Zhou, *Cishan zhi*, 46, 479.

16. 1881 *Guangde zhouzhi* 13/11ff.; 1875 *Longyang xianzhi* 8/18; 1201–4 *Jiatai Wuxing zhi*.

17. 1456 *Huan yu tongzhi* 8/3, 11, 20. Following the precedent of the Liu Song dynasty and on the foundations of the academy it had built there in the middle of the fifth century, the Ming dynasty had in 1381 built the Guozijian (Imperial Academy) there, as well as ten temples. The 1461 *(Da) Ming yitong zhi* 6/26 records that deity Zhang Bo was granted a temple in Guangde county in 1388. On the relationship between the two national gazetteers, see Goodrich and Fang, *Dictionary of Ming Biography*, 1019. For more on this deity, especially in Guangde, see Hansen, *Changing Gods in Medieval China*, 148–52, and Guo, *Exorcism and Money*, 60–84.

18. Zhou and Zhou, *Cishan zhi*.

19. Song Na, "Chi jian Cishan Guanghui ci ji" 敕建祠山廣惠祠記, in his *Xiyin ji* 5/21b.

20. For the god's origins in the Huzhou area, see for example 1881 *Guangde zhouzhi* 13/11ff; 1875 *Longyang xianzhi* 8/18; 1201–4 *Jiatai Wuxing zhi*. The *Guangde zhouzhi* mentions that he may instead have come from Longyang county in Changde prefecture, Hunan, but the 1535 *Changde fuzhi* 10/8 rejects this explanation of its local Zhanggong temple. For his mother, see *Ming tongzhi*, cited in 1875 *Longyang xianzhi*. For his wife and daughters, see Zhao, *Gaiyu congkao*, j. 35 "Cishan shen." For the Song festival, see Zhou, *Qidong yeyu*, j. 13; Wu, *Meng liang lu*, j. 1. For Yixing, see *Huang Ming siguan zhi*, 34; the anonymous author notes that the reason there are so many temples in that county is that the god had once undertaken some work there. I suspect either the author or the copyist (who I think did not copy everything) of being from Yixing because there is so much more information on Yixing than elsewhere, and because only Yixing is indexed on the fold of the page. *Guangde zhouzhi* 13/15. As part of the high Ming movement to destroy so-called improper shrines (see Schneewind, "Competing Institutions," and Schneewind, *Community Schools and the State*), in 1525 Zou Shouyi mounted a vain attack on the cult of Cishan's consort 1881.

21. Campany, *Strange Writing*, 369–70.

22. 1496 *Jurong xianzhi* 1/7 (351).

23. On this process, see Hansen, *Changing Gods in Medieval China*. Many individual cults have now also been studied. Worship might express the worshipper's desire for contact, as when Taizu asked Cishan for a sign. The Han emperor Wu (Han Wudi), for instance, had brought two jade gifts to the beautiful and powerful deity Queen Mother of the West. She had descended to him on five-colored clouds, and ever after, missing her, he built a shrine wherever such clouds were seen. *Huang Ming siguan zhi*, 18?; Goodall, *Heaven and Earth*, 18.

24. 1881 *Guangde zhouzhi* 23/22a, citing Zhou Bingxiu 周秉秀, *Cishan shiyao* 祠山事要 (1239).

25. In 1447, repairs were ordered, and two years later they were stopped because they were "not an urgent task." *Ming Yingzong shilu*

for Zhengtong 14, tenth month, 30/184/3614. The petition for repairs came from Vice Censor-in-Chief Cui Gong (who at the time was overseeing Suzhou and Songjiang). The Qing comment comes from Zhao, *Gaiyu congkao*, last comment in j. 35 "Cishan shen." The exchange of treasures is from Xu, "Cishan qibao" (The seven treasures of Cishan), 24/6 (5/653).

26. 1750/1900 *Jurong xianzhi*, 1157. The petition does not appear in the *Veritable Records* for that year.

27. 1496 *Jurong xianzhi* 1/8 (351), 5/27b (399). 1676 *Jurong xianzhi* 1/22 (121), 2/32 (65).

28. 1750/1900 *Jurong xianzhi* 4/25–26. The 1496 gazetteer lists three other Cishan temples in other districts (5/17, 5/28b, 5/29b). According to one writer, Jurong people had had temples to King Zhang at least since the Tang period, and at least eight were scattered all over the county. Cheng, "Jurong yishi lu," part 2, 125–29. Further recent accounts of the Zhang temple in *Jurong diming qutan* try to tie the mixed-up records of the past into neat packages. Niu Fenghua 牛风华 and Cao Li 曹丽, in "Gujin Zhangmiao" 古今张庙, argue that the Zhang temple was the same as the Qianguang Zen temple, because both are listed as having been located 10 *li* south of town (125–27). I could find no other documentary evidence for this contention. Qin Jinbao 秦今寶, in "Diming yu mingren" 地名與名人, writes that Zhang Bo was a descendant of the ancient Zhang Bing 張秉 who had helped the mythical sage-king Yu manage the waters, and that Bing and Bo were worshipped in Jurong together after Bo had been buried on the spot (174).

29. 1750/1900 *Jurong xianzhi*, 1158–59.

30. The saying is reported in Zhang, " 'Zhang' xing yu 'Jurong cheng' " (The Zhang clan and Jurong city), in *Jurong ribao* (Jurong daily news), May 2, 1997. In May, 2004, Zhang Qingwen 張慶文, a journalist in his thirties, said that he vividly remembered reading this article in the 1990s sometime. When I complimented Mr. Zhang on remembering the story for so long, he said that naturally he had been pleased to see a story about his family in the newspaper and that moreover it had been written by his late teacher Zhang Caiguang. After much searching, the article was found after I had returned to the United States. Zhang Qingwen also pointed out that Jurong, as the gateway to Nanjing, is a county of immigrants that has lost and

gained populations several times (making the continuity of the Zhangs all the more unusual).

31. 1750/1900 *Jurong xianzhi* 1158–60 (10/30–32).

32. Zhai Zhonghua, personal communication, May 7, 2004. Village head Zhang Yuansheng 張元生 remembered the couplet as "In the Tang dynasty loyal and filial sons, in the Liang and Tang a family of prime ministers" 唐代忠孝子, 梁唐宰相家. Both personal communication, May 7, 2004.

Chapter VI (see pp. 70–90)

1. Lee, *Celebration of Continuity*, 1–2.

2. Chan, "The Rise of Ming T'ai-tsu," 710–11.

3. Liu Song, in Dardess, *A Ming Society*, 16.

4. *Shi jing*, Legge, trans., *The She King, or the Book of Poetry*, 437ff. See also Waley's translation, 240.

5. Lee, *Celebration of Continuity*, 27.

6. Ho, "Plant Symbolism in the Religious Poems of the *Book of Poetry*," 166.

7. *Yitai Zhang shi jiasheng* (Genealogy of the Yitai Zhang).

8. Zhu, *The Placard of People's Instructions* (1398), translated in Farmer, *Zhu Yuanzhang and Early Ming Legislation*, 202. For a discussion of the *Da Gao*, and translations of many of its passages, see Dardess, *Confucianism and Autocracy*, chapter 4.

9. See de Bary et al., *Sources of Chinese Tradition*, vol. 2, 70–71, 125–26.

10. Ming Xuanzong (the Xuande emperor), *The Book of the Five Relationships* (*Wulun shu*). Goodrich and Fang, *Dictionary of Ming Biography*, 293, 970. The date of publication of the *Book of the Five Relationships* is unclear. One of the *DMB* articles gives 1443, the other 1448. Brook, "Edifying Knowledge," 106, lists works distributed to county schools. Working out which books school libraries purchased and which were bestowed by the central government, Brook notes

that Cili county's copy of this text was not "'issued' until 1447, four years after it was published." He concludes that the time gap may mean money had to be raised to buy the book (106). But the preface to the *Book of the Five Relationships* is dated 1447. (See also Brook, "Communications and Commerce," 652.) The text covers each of the five bilateral relationships (ruler-minister, father-son, husband-wife, elder and younger brother, and friends), but of 62 chapters, 53 are on the first, and moreover the ruler and minister sections are oddly disjoined. The section headings are: "Jun dao" (Way of the ruler; 22 chapters), "Chen dao" (Way of the minister; 20 chapters), "Fu dao" (Way of the father; 2 chapters), "Zi dao" (Way of the son; 3 chapters); "Fu fu zhi dao" (Way of husband and wife; 1 chapter), "Xiongdi zhi dao" (Way of brothers; 1 chapter), and "Pengyou" (friends; 2 chapters). Whereas the latter three topics are really about relationships, rulers, ministers, fathers, and sons are each granted separate sections. The ruler, after all, does not relate only to his ministers: his responsibility is broader, to Heaven and to the people, and in the case of the melons particularly, the relation to the ministers is only one element. Each section is further divided into paired manifestations of the proper way—*jia yan* 嘉言 and *shan xing* 善行 (good speech and good behavior)—expressions that go back to the *Book of Documents* and the *Record of Rites* respectively, and that were used together by the Song period (*Hanyu da cidian*, 441, 475). Within each of those there are then more specific types of virtue. Since the five relationships are the fundamental building blocks of morality, the book promises a complete typology of Confucian virtue.

11. There are half a dozen minor word changes and three omissions in the *Book of the Five Relationships*. The name of the building where the audience took place, which appears in both the essay and the *Veritable Records*, is omitted, presumably as irrelevant to an audience outside the capital. Liu Yan (see below) (and the responsible compiler, if it was not Liu) must have had Taizu's text as well, because the *Book of the Five Relationships* includes the emperor's ode, which the *Veritable Records* does not, and because Liu's poem includes the emperor's ode's good wish for Zhang Guan. The only differences in the ode are two erroneous characters in the gazetteer version of the *Book of the Five Relationships* version of the emperor's ode.

12. A list of important local events in the 1904 gazetteer does include, for 1433 and 1456, Zhang Jian's mourning for his parents

and the auspicious omens that resulted, but it says nothing about the presentation of the melons and the execution of Jian's grandfather and great-uncle. 1904 *Xucuan Jurong xianzhi* 2 middle/8.

13. Zhang Hui passed the first examination in Chenghua 6, the year before Zhang Jian died. 1496 *Jurong xianzhi* 6/26.

14. 1904 *Xucuan Jurong xianzhi* 18/23. The group of four poems, including Zhang's, appears in the 1496 *Jurong xianzhi*.

15. Liu, *The Poetry of Li Shang-yin*, 141.

16. In the Han period, Shao Ping, the Marquis of Eastern Mound (Dongling), lost his wealth and his title, and ended up raising melons. Fortunately, they were extremely good melons. A poem by Tao Yuanming (365–427) celebrates the former marquis's reclusive and peaceful life: "Shaoping working in his field of melons/Was as much as he had been when Lord of Dongling." (Translation by William Acker, in Minford and Lau, eds., *Classical Chinese Literature*, p. 502.)

17. Ni, "Yishan xiansheng Zhang gong ai ci, bing xu."

18. Ni, "Yishan xiansheng Zhang gong ai ci, bing xu."

19. Liu Yan 劉儼, "Jia gua shi" 嘉瓜詩, in 1750/1900 *Jurong xianzhi* 10/51a (1261).

20. Song Lian, "Hymn on Auspicious Melons."

21. Xue Xuan, "Shu *Jia gua ji* hou" 書嘉瓜集后, in *Xue Xuan wenji*, 638–39.

22. Wu Jie 吳節, "Jia gua shi" 嘉瓜詩, in 1750/1900 *Jurong xianzhi* 10/51a (1261).

23. Xue, "Shu *Jia gua ji* hou" 638–39.

24. Li Ling, "Jia gua fu" 嘉瓜賦, in *Li Gongzhan wenji*, 1/15–16. It is even possible that Zhang Jian lobbied for incorporation of the story into the *Book of the Five Relationships* in the early years of his career.

25. Huang, *Hanli ji* 11/15.

26. Huang, *Hanli ji* 11/15.

27. Dardess, *A Ming Society*, 229. The Great Ritual Controversy of the Ming period should not be confused with the later "Rites

Controversy" between Jesuit missionaries and their Catholic opponents of other orders over whether Christianity could accommodate Chinese ancestor worship.

28. Dardess, *A Ming Society*, 229.

29. Bloom, "The Moral Autonomy of the Individual in Confucian Tradition," 26.

30. Ditmanson, "Huang Zuo and the Construction of Late Ming Nostalgia."

31. Shen, *Wanli yehuo bian*, 923–24.

32. Ibid.

33. Ibid.

34. Zhu, *Huang Ming shi gai* 5/6/17. Perhaps this kind of adept switch accounts for Tao Kai's political survival. For another account of the *Huiyao* proposal, unconnected with melons, see Zhang, *Huang Ming tongji zhijie* 2/38b–40a. For another Ming account of the melon audience based on the *Veritable Records*, see *Guochao jiyao* 1/45.

35. Zhong Xing, *Ming ji nian bian* 1/27.

36. Zhang, *Guoshi jiwen* 2/87.

37. Originally published in 1603 by Wang Qi, the compilation was extended under the Qianlong emperor as *Qinding xu wenxian tongkao*. It includes the melons in its category "vegetable anomalies" (*cao yi* 草異), distinguished from "tree anomalies" and "grain anomalies" and other kinds filling 13 *juan* (chapters) of the Qing work (schools, by comparison, get only 4 *juan*, ancestral temples 5). The brief record (39 characters) mentions Jurong twice. Zhang Guan's style name, Gubin, does not appear in the accounts by Taizu, Song Lian, and Huang Zuo, or in the *Veritable Records*, so Wang Qi (and Jiao Hong) must have been looking at the Jurong gazetteer, Ni Qian's epitaph for Zhang Yi, or another source. *Qinding xu wenxian tongkao* j. 218.

38. Cheng, "Jurong yishi lu," 128.

39. Ibid.

40. Jurong difangzhi bangongshe, *Jurong minjian gushi*, 50–51.

41. Xia, "Waiguo xuezhe qingxi Jurong shizhi," 38.

42. Chen, "Jurong xiancheng diming yanbian qianshi," 58–61.

43. Zhang Caibo, telephone interview by Wen Dezhong, May 9, 2004. Mr Zhang is of Dai village, Biancheng township.

44. Wen Dezhong, personal communication by fax and e-mail, July 1, 2004 and July 9, 2004.

45. 1904 *Xucuan Jurong xianzhi* 16/11–12 reports that the stele for Zhang Jian on the Righteous Mound still exists, and Yang Shiyuan discusses the state of the steles and copies the epitaph in his *Jurong jinshi ji* 7/33a–35b. Yang also worked on the steles section of the 1904 gazetteer.

46. A Han period woman buried in about 160 BCE was excavated in 1972, so well preserved by layers of cloth and wood that an autopsy was performed, which found her to have a stomach full of melon seeds. Cheng, "Evidence of Type A Personality in a Chinese Lady Who Died of Acute Myocardial Infarction 2,100 Years Ago," 154–55, referring to his excavation reported in *National Geographic* 145 (1974): 660–81.

47. Details on this building and its rediscovery are in the 1994 *Jurong xianzhi*. It is now in the care of the county museum. The degree to which the clan flourished and grew can be seen in the wide disparity between generation and age. For instance, journalist Zhang Qingwen was of two generations earlier than his late teacher, Zhang Caiguang, according to the list of generational characters given me by Wen Dezhong, whose maternal grandfather came from this Zhang family (personal communication, May 6, 2004).

Works Cited[*]

1456 *Huan yu tongzhi* 寰宇通志. (Gazetteer for the whole empire). Peng Shi 彭時, Ni Qian 倪謙, et al., eds. Reprint Nanjing: Guoli tushuguan, 1947.

1461 *(Da) Ming yitong zhi* 大明一統志. (Gazetteer for the whole empire). Li Xian 李賢 et al., eds. Reprinted in *Siku quanshu*, Taipei: Taiwan shangwu yinshuguan, 1983.

1534 *Jiajing Nanji zhi* 嘉靖南畿志. (Gazetteer for the southern capital area, called Nanzhili). Wen Renchuan 聞人詮 et al., eds. Reprint Taiwan: Xuesheng shuju, 1987.

1577 *Yingtian fuzhi* 應天府志. (Gazetteer for Yingtian prefecture, Nanzhili). Wang Yihua 王一化 et al., eds.

1496 *Jurong xianzhi* 句容縣志. (Gazetteer for Jurong county, Nanzhili). 王僖 et al., eds. Reprinted in Tianyige series, 1964.

1676 *Jurong xianzhi* 句容縣志. (Gazetteer for Jurong county).

1750/1900 *Jurong xianzhi* 句容縣志. (Gazetteer for Jurong county). Cao Xixian 曹襲先 and later Yang Shiyuan 楊世沅 eds.

1904 *Xuzuan Jurong xianzhi* 續纂句容縣志. (Continuation of gazetteer for Jurong county). Zhang Shaotang 張紹棠 et al., eds.

1994 *Jurong xianzhi* 句容縣志. (Gazetteer for Jurong county). Nanjing: Jiangsu renmin chubanshe.

1810/1817 *Chongxiu Yangzhou fuzhi* 重修揚州府志 (Revised gazetteer for Yangzhou prefecture, in Nanzhili in Ming period).

1881 *Guangde zhouzhi* 光德州志. (Gazetteer for Guangde subprefecture, in Nanzhili in Ming period). Hu Youcheng 胡有誠 et al., eds. Reprint Nanjing: Jiangsu guji chubanshe, 1998.

Entries marked * may be suitable for undergraduate classes.
Entries marked ** include substantial primary sources in translation.

1201–4 *Jiatai Wuxing zhi* 嘉泰吳興志 (Gazetteer for Wuxing, Huzhou, Zhejiang province, from Song dynasty, Jiatai period). Tan Yao 談鑰, ed. Reprint Shanghai: Shanghai guji chubanshe, 1995–99.

1535 *Changde fuzhi* 常德府志 (Gazetteer for Changde prefecture, in Huguang province in Ming period). Chen Hongmo 陳洪謨 et al., eds.

1875 *Longyang xianzhi* 龍陽縣志. (Gazetteer for Longyang county, in Changde prefecture in Huguang province in Ming period). Huang Wentong 黃文桐 et al., eds. Reprint Nanjing: Jiangsu guji chubanshe, 2002.

1604 *Laizhou fuzhi* 萊州府志 (Gazetteer for Laizhou prefecture, Shandong). Zhao Yao 趙燿, ed. Reprint Qingdao: Donglai Zhou shi Yong hou tang, 1939.

1735 *Shaanxi tongzhi* 陝西通志 (Gazetteer for Shaanxi province). Liu Yuyi 劉於義 et al., eds. Reprinted in *Siku quanshu*, electronic version.

1555 *Guizhou tongzhi* 貴州通志 (Gazetteer for Guizhou province). Xie Dongshan 謝東山 et al., eds. Reprinted in Tianyige series, 1990.

1741 *Guizhou tongzhi* 貴州通志 (Gazetteer for Guizhou province). E'ertai 鄂爾泰 et al., eds. Reprinted in *Siku quanshu*, electronic version.

Bloom, Irene. "The Moral Autonomy of the Individual in Confucian Tradition." In William C. Kirby, ed., *Realms of Freedom in Modern China*. Stanford: Stanford University Press, 2004.

** Boxer, C. R. *South China in the Sixteenth Century*. London: Hakluyt Society, 1953.

*Bray, Francesca. *Technology and Gender: Fabrics of Power in Late Imperial China*. Berkeley: University of California Press, 1997.

Brokaw, Cynthia J. *Ledgers of Merit and Demerit: Social Order and Moral Order in Late Imperial China*. Princeton: Princeton University Press, 1991.

*Brook, Timothy. *The Confusions of Pleasure: Commerce and Culture in Ming China*. Berkeley: University of California Press, 1998.

Brook, Timothy. "Edifying Knowledge: The Building of School Libraries in Ming China." *Late Imperial China* 17.1 (1996): 93–116.

Brook, Timothy. "Communications and Commerce." In Twitchett and Mote, *The Cambridge History of China, Volume 8*.

Campany, Robert Ford. *Strange Writing: Anomaly Accounts in Early Medieval China*. Albany: State University of New York Press, 1996.

*Cass, Victoria. *Dangerous Women: Warriors, Grannies, and Geishas of the Ming*. Lanham, MD: Rowman and Littlefield, 1999.

Chan, Hok-Lam. "The Chien-wen, Yung-lo, Hung-hsi, and Hsüan-te Reigns, 1399–1435." In Mote and Twitchett, *The Cambridge History of China, Volume 7*.

Chan, Hok-Lam. "The Rise of Ming T'ai-tsu (1368–1398): Facts and Fictions in Early Ming Official Historiography." *Journal of the American Oriental Society* 95.4 (1975): 679–715.

**Chan, Hok-Lam. "Xie Jin (1369–1415) as an Imperial Propagandist: His Role in the Revisions of the *Ming Taizu Shilu*." *T'oung Pao* 91: 58–124.

Chen Tian 陳田 (1848–1921). *Ming shi jishi* 明诗記事. Facsimile reprint, Taiwan: Zhonghua shuju, 1971.

Chen Xiangchen 陳相臣. "Jurong xiancheng diming yanbian qianshi" 句容縣城地名演變淺釋. *Jurong wenshi ziliao* 11 (1993): 58–61.

Cheng, Anne. "What Did It Mean to be a *Ru* in Han Times?" *Asia Major*, 3rd ser., 14.2 (2001): 101–18.

Cheng, Tsung O. "Evidence of Type A Personality in a Chinese Lady Who Died of Acute Myocardial Infarction 2,100 Years Ago." *Texas Heart Institute Journal* 29.2 (2002): 154–55.

Cheng Zunping 程尊平. "Jurong yishi lu" 句容軼事錄. Part 2. *Jurong wenshi ziliao* 句容文史資料 8 (October 1990): 125–29.

Cleaves, Francis Woodman. "The Memorial for Presenting the
   Yuan Shih." *Asia Major*, 3rd ser., 1.1 (1988): 59–69.

da Cruz, Gaspar. "Treatise in Which the Things of China Are
   Related at Great Length. . . ." Translated in Boxer, *South China
   in the Sixteenth Century.* Originally published in Portuguese
   c. 1569.

*Dardess, John W. *Confucianism and Autocracy: Professional Elites in
   the Founding of the Ming Dynasty.* Berkeley: University of
   California Press, 1983.

*Dardess, John W. *A Ming Society: T'ai-ho County, Jiangxi,
   Fourteenth to Seventeenth Centuries.* Berkeley: University of
   California Press, 1996.

de Bary, W^m. Theodore, et al. *Sources of Chinese Tradition.* 2nd ed.
   New York: Columbia University Press, 2000.

de Crespigny, Rafe. *Portents of Protest in the Later Han Dynasty.*
   Canberra: Australian National University Press, 1976.

de Rada, Fr. Martin, O.E.S.A. *Relation of the Things of China,
   Which Is Properly Called Taybin.* Translated in Boxer, *South China
   in the Sixteenth Century.* Originally published in Latin,
   1575–1576.

Ditmanson, Peter. "Huang Zuo and the Construction of Late
   Ming Nostalgia." Paper presented at the Association of Asian
   Studies conference, San Diego, CA, March 10, 2000. Cited by
   permission.

*Dreyer, Edward L. *Early Ming China: A Political History,
   1355–1435.* Stanford: Stanford University Press, 1982.

Eberhard, Wolfram. "The Political Function of Astronomy and
   Astronomers in Han China." In John K. Fairbank, ed., *Chinese
   Thought and Institutions.* Chicago: University of Chicago Press,
   1957.

Elman, Benjamin. *A Cultural History of Civil Examinations in Late
   Imperial China.* Berkeley: University of California Press, 2000.

*Elvin, Mark. "Female Virtue and the State in China." *Past and
   Present* 104 (1984): 111–52.

Elvin, Mark. "Who Was Responsible for the Weather?" *Osiris* 13 (1998): 213–37.

Farmer, Edward. *Early Ming Government: The Evolution of Dual Capitals.* Cambridge: East Asian Research Center, Harvard University, 1976.

**Farmer, Edward. *Zhu Yuanzhang and Early Ming Legislation: The Reordering of Chinese Society Following the Era of Mongol Rule.* Leiden: E.J. Brill, 1995. Includes translations of many documents written by Ming Taizu.

**Feng Zikai. "Eating Melon Seeds." Translated in David Pollard, ed., *The Chinese Essay.* New York: Columbia University Press, 2000. Originally published in Chinese in 1934.

**Feng Menglong. "Old Man Zhang Grows Melons and Marries Wennu." Translated in Shuhui Yang and Yunqin Yang, *Stories Old and New: A Ming Dynasty Collection.* Seattle: University of Washington Press, 2000. The story is translated as "The Fairy's Rescue" in a much smaller collection: Cyril Birch, trans. **Stories from a Ming Collection.* New York: Grove Press, 1958, 1999.

Franke, Wolfgang. "Historical Writing during the Ming." In Mote and Twitchett, *Cambridge History of China, Volume 7.*

Goodrich, L. Carrington and Chaoying Fang, eds. *Dictionary of Ming Biography.* New York: Columbia University Press, 1976.

Guochao jiyao 國朝紀要. 1968 Hishi copy of Ming original, in Princeton University library.

*Guo, Qitao. *Exorcism and Money: The Symbolic World of the Five-Fury Spirits in Late Imperial China.* Berkeley: Institute of Asian Studies, University of California, 2003.

Guo Tingxun 過廷訓. *Benchao fensheng renwu kao* 本朝分省人物考 (Study of men of our dynasty, divided by province). 1622. Facsimile reprint in 30 vols., Taipei, Chengwen chubanshe, 1971.

Han Yu 韓愈 (768–824). *Han Changli wenji jiaozhu* 韓昌黎校注. Taipei: Shijie shuju, 1967.

*Hansen, Valerie. *Changing Gods in Medieval China.* Princeton: Princeton University Press, 1990.

He Chuguang 何出光. *Lantai fa jian lu* 蘭臺法鑒錄, 1597.

Heijdra, Martin. "The Socio-Economic Development of Ming Rural China (1368–1644)." Ph.D. diss., Princeton University, 1994.

*Ho, Shun-yee. "Plant Symbolism in the Religious Poems of the *Book of Poetry.*" *Journal of Oriental Studies* 37.2 (1999): 163–72.

Ho, Yün-yi. "Ideological Implications of Major Sacrifices in Early Ming." *Ming Studies* 6 (1978): 55–73.

Huang Ming siguan zhi 皇明寺觀志. Ming dynasty after 1492; Qing hand copy. Held in Nanjing Library.

Hucker, Charles O. *A Dictionary of Official Titles in Imperial China.* Stanford: Stanford University Press, 1985.

Hucker, Charles O. "Ming Government." In Twitchett and Mote, *Cambridge History of China, Volume 8.*

*Huang, Ray. *1587: A Year of No Significance.* New Haven: Yale University Press, 1981.

Huang Zuo 黃佐. *Hanli ji* 翰林記 (Record of the Hanlin Academy). *Siku quanshu* electronic edition. Originally published in 1541.

Jiang Baochai 江寶釵, ed. *Mianmian si yuan dao: Yuefu shi xuancui* 綿綿思遠道: 樂府詩選粹. Taipei: Youshi wenhua shiye gongsi, 1991.

**Jiang, Yonglin, trans. *The Great Ming Code (Da Ming Lü* 大明律*).* Seattle: University of Washington Press, 2005. Originally published in Chinese in 1397.

Jiao Hong 焦竑. (1541–1620) *Guochao xianzheng lu* 國朝獻徵錄.

Jurong diming qutan 句容地名趣談 (Discussion of place names in Jurong). Jurong: Jurong shizheng ban xuexi he wenshi weiyuanhui, 2003.

Jurong difangzhi bangongshe, ed. *Jurong minjian gushi* 句容民間故事 (Folk stories of Jurong). Nanjing: Jiangsu guji chubanshe, 2001.

Jurong xian diming weiyuanhui (Committee on place names of Jurong county). *Jiangsu sheng Jurong xian diming lu* 江苏省句容县地名录. Jurong: Jurong diming weiyuanhui, 1983.

*Kutcher, Norman. *Mourning in Late Imperial China: Filial Piety and the State*. New York: Cambridge University Press, 1999.

*Laing, Ellen Johnston. *Art and Aesthetics in Chinese Popular Prints: Selections from the Muban Foundation Collection*. Ann Arbor: Center for Chinese Studies, University of Michigan, 2002.

Langlois, John D., Jr. "The Hung-wu Reign." In Mote and Twitchett, *Cambridge History of China, Volume 7*.

*Lederose, Lotthar. *Ten Thousand Things: Module and Mass Production in Chinese Art*. Princeton: Princeton University Press, 2000.

Lee, Peter H. *Celebration of Continuity: Themes in Classic East Asian Poetry*. Cambridge, MA: Harvard University Press, 1979.

***Li ji* 禮記 (Record of Rites). Translated by James Legge. 1895. Reprint, Delhi: Motilal Banardidass, 1966.

Li Ling 李齡 (fl. 1429–67). *Li Gongzhan wenji* 李宮詹文集. Reprinted in *Chaozhou qijiu ji* 潮州耆舊集.

Li Tang 李唐. *Ming Taizu*. Hong Kong: Hongye shuju chubanshe, 1961.

Liu Chen 劉辰. *Guochu shiji* 國初事蹟 (Traces of events from the beginning of the dynasty). Yongle-era; reprinted in *Zhongguo yeshi jicheng* 中國野史集成, Chengdu: Ba Shu shushe, 1993.

Liu, James J. Y. *The Poetry of Li Shang-yin: Ninth-Century Baroque Chinese Poet*. Chicago: University of Chicago Press, 1969.

**Liu Jung-en. *Six Yuan Plays*. London: Penguin Books, 1972.

Loewe, Michael. "China." In Michael Loewe and Carmen Blacker, eds., *Oracles and Divination*. Boulder: Shambala Publications, 1981.

Loewe, Michael. "The Cycle of Cathay: Concepts of Time in Han China and Their Problems." In Chun-chieh Huang and Erik Zürcher, eds., *Time and Space in Chinese Culture*, 305–28. Leiden: Brill, 1995.

Lippiello, Tiziana. *Auspicious Omens and Miracles in Ancient China: Han, Three Kingdoms, and Six Dynasties.* Monumenta Serica Monograph Series, no. 39. Saint Augustin: Monumenta Serica Institute, 2001.

Lu Rong 陸容. *Shuyuan zaji* 菽園雜記. 1494. Reprint Beijing: Zhonghua shuju, 1985.

**John Minford and Joseph S.M. Lau, eds., *Classical Chinese Literature: an Anthology of Translations.* New York: Columbia University Press, 2000.

Ming Taizu shilu, see *Veritable Records.*

Ming Xuanzong. *Wulun shu* 五倫書 *(Book of the Five Relationships).*

*Miyazaki, Ichisada. *China's Examination Hell.* Translated by Conrad Schirokauer. New Haven: Yale University Press, 1976.

Mote, Frederick W. "The Rise of the Ming Dynasty, 1330–1367." In Mote and Twitchett, eds., *The Cambridge History of China: Volume 7.*

Mote, Frederick W. and Denis Twitchett, eds. *The Cambridge History of China, Volume 7: The Ming Dynasty, 1368–1644, Part One.* Cambridge: Cambridge University Press, 1988.

Nanjing Xiaoling Bowuguan. *Ming Xiaoling zhi xinbian* 明孝陵志新編 (Gazetteer of the Ming filial tomb, new edition). Harbin: Heilongjiang renmin chubanshe, 2002.

Ni Qian 倪謙 (1415–1479). "Yishan xiansheng Zhang gong ai ci bing xu" 已山先生張公哀辭并序. In his *Ni wenxi ji* 倪文僖集. *Siku quanshu* electronic edition.

Nicholson, Adam. *God's Secretaries: The Making of the King James Bible.* New York: Perennial, 2004.

Nivison, David S. "Aspects of Traditional Chinese Biography." *Journal of Asian Studies* 21.4 (1962): 457–63. Reprint with permission of the Association of Asian Studies, Inc.

Qian Bocheng 錢伯城 et al., eds. *Quan Ming wen* 全明文 (Complete Ming Writings). Shanghai: Shanghai guji chubanshe, 1992.

Rao Longsun 饶龙隼. "Mingchu shiwen de zouxiang" 明初诗文的走向 (Trends in early Ming literature). *Journal of Jiangxi Normal University "Jianxi shifan daxue xuebao"* 江西师范大学学报 34.2 (May 2001).

Rossabi, Morris. "Ming Foreign Policy: The Case of Hami." In Sabine Dabringhaus and Roderich Ptak, eds., *China and Her Neighbors: Borders, Visions of the Other, Foreign Policy, Tenth to Nineteenth Century.* Wiesbaden: Harrassowitz Verlag, 1997.

Schneewind, Sarah. *Community Schools and the State in Ming China.* Stanford: Stanford University Press, 2006.

Schneewind, Sarah. "Competing Institutions: Community Schools and 'Improper Shrines' in Sixteenth-Century China." *Late Imperial China* 20.1 (1999): 85–106.

Schneewind, Sarah. "Visions and Revisions: Village Policies of the Ming Founder in Seven Phases." *T'oung Pao* 87 (2002): 1–43.

Shang Lu 商輅 (1414–1486). "Taipu Zhang gong shendao bei" 太僕張公神道碑. In 1496 *Jurong xianzhi* 531 (11/63–64). The full title, given by Yang Shiyuan, who copied the inscription into his collection (*q.V.*), was "Taizhong dafu taipu siqing Zhang gong shendao beiming."

Shen Defu 沈德符. *Wanli yehuo bian* 萬歷野獲編. 1619. Reprint, Beijing: Zhonghua shudian, 1997.

Shen Yue 沈約 (441–513). *Song shu* 宋書 (History of the Liu Song Dynasty). Reprint, Beijing: Zhonghua shuju, 1974.

**Shi jing* 詩經 (also called *Book of Poetry, Book of Songs,* and *Classic of Odes*). Translated in James Legge, *The She King, or the Book of Poetry.* Reprint, Hong Kong: Hong Kong University Press, 1970. There are many other translations, including those by Arthur Waley and Ezra Pound.

*Smedley, Agnes. *The Great Road: The Life and Times of Chu Te.* New York: Monthly Review Press, 1956.

Song Lian 宋濂, Jia gua song 嘉瓜頌 (Hymn on Auspicious Melons) in *(Huang) Ming Wenheng* 19/8–9. Siku quanshu electronic edition. Also in his *Luanpo houji.*

Song Na 宋訥 (1311–1390). *Xiyin ji* 西隱集. Siku quanshu edition.

Strickmann, Michel. "The Maoshan Revelations: Taoism and the Aristocracy." *T'oung Pao* 63 (1977): 1–64.

Sun Zhengrong 孫正容. *Zhu Yuanzhang xinian yaolu* 朱元璋系年要錄. Hangzhou: Zhejiang renmin chubanshe, 1983.

Tan Qian 談遷 (1594–1657). *Zaolin zazu* 棗林雜俎. Reprint, Taibei: Xinxing shuju, 1962. (In *Biji xiaoshuo daguan*. vol. 2, 1599–787).

**Taylor, Romeyn. "Ming T'ai-tsu's Story of a Dream." *Monumenta Serica* 32 (1976): 1–20.

**Thompson, Laurence G. *Chinese Religion: An Introduction* (third edition). Belmont: Wadsworth, 1979.

**Thompson, Laurence G. *The Chinese Way in Religion*. Belmont: Wadsworth Publishing, 1973.

*Tsai, Shih-shan Henry. *Perpetual Happiness: The Ming Emperor Yongle*. Seattle: University of Washington Press, 2001.

Twitchett, Denis. *The Writing of Official History under the Tang*. Cambridge: Cambridge University Press, 1992.

Twitchett, Denis and Frederick W. Mote, eds. *The Cambridge History of China, Volume 8: The Ming Dynasty, 1368–1644, Part Two*. Cambridge: Cambridge University Press, 1998.

Veritable Records of the Reign of Ming Taizu (*Ming Taizu shilu* 明太祖實錄). In *Ming shilu*, facsimile reproduction of Guoli Beiping tushuguan cang hong'ge chaoben, 133 vols. Taibei: Zhongyang yanjiuyuan lishi yuyan yanjiusuo, 1961–1966.

Wakefield, David. *Household Division and Inheritance in Qing and Republican China*. Honolulu: University of Hawaii Press, 1998.

Wan Sitong 萬斯同 (1638–1702). *Mingshi chaoben* 明史抄本 (A draft of the Ming History).

Wang Qi 王圻 (*jinshi* 1565, 1565–1614), ed. *Qinding xu wenxian tongkao* 欽定文獻通考. 1603. Additions made under the Qianlong emperor (1736–1795).

Wang Qi 王圻, ed. *San cai tuhui* 三才圖會 1607. Facsimile reprint, Taibei: Chengwen chubanshe, 1970. Parts of this text have been translated by John Goodall as **Heaven and Earth: Leaves from a Ming Encyclopedia. Boulder: Shambala Press, 1979.

Wu, Hung. The Wu Liang Shrine: The Ideology of Early Chinese Pictorial Art. Stanford: Stanford University Press, 1989.

Wu Zimu 吳自牧 (fl. c. 1276). Meng liang lu 夢粱錄.

Xia Qiyun 夏啓云. "Waiguo xuezhe qingxi Jurong shizhi" 外國學者情係句容史志 (Foreign scholars interested in Jurong historical gazetteers). Jiangxi difangzhi 江苏地方志 (Jiangsu Local Chronicles) (2004): 38.

Xi'an shi wenwu baohu kaogu suo 西安市文物保護考古所. "Xi'an nanjiao huang Ming zongshi Qianyang Duanyi wang Zhu gong Zeng mu qingli jianbao" 西安市南郊皇明宗室沔陽端懿王朱公金曾墓清理簡報. Kaogu yu wenwu 考古文物 6 (2001): 29–45.

Xie Jin 解縉 (1369–1415). See also Veritable Records.

Xie Jin. Wenyi ji 文毅集. 1457 (and later editions). Reprinted in Siku quanshu zhenben, Taibei: Taiwan shangwu yinshuguan, 1973.

*Xiaoling Museum of Nanjing. Xiaoling Tomb of the Ming Dynasty. Nanjing: H.K. International Publishing House, 2002. Includes photographs of Taizu's tomb.

Xu Yingqiu 徐應秋 (jinshi 1616). "Cishan qibao" 祠山七寶 (The seven treasures of Cishan). In his Yu zhi tang tanhui 玉芝堂談薈. (24/6), Reprinted in Biji xiaoshuo daguan 筆記小説大觀, vol. 5, p. 653. Yangzhou: Jiangsu Guangling guji keyinshe, 1995.

Xue Xuan 薛瑄 (1389–1464). Xue Xuan wenji 薛瑄文集. Reprint, Taiyuan: Shanxi renmin chubanshe, 1990.

Yang Shiyuan 楊世沅. Jurong jinshi ji 句容金石記 c. 1900.

Yang Yifan 楊一凡. Ming Da Gao yanjiu 明大誥研究 (Research on the Ming Great Warning). Nanjing: Jiangsu renmin chubanshe, 1988.

Yitai Zhang shi jiasheng 義臺張氏家乘 (Genealogy of the Yitai Zhang clan). 1902; reprint Jurong: s.n., 2005.

Zhao Yi 趙翼 (1727–1814). Gaiyu congkao 陔餘叢考.

Zhang Caiguang 張才光. "'Zhang' xing yu 'Jurong cheng'" 張姓與句容城 (The Zhang clan and Jurong city). *Jurong ribao* 句容日報 (Jurong daily news), May 2, 1997.

Zhang Jiahe 張嘉和. *Huang Ming tongji zhijie* 皇明通紀直解. c. 1645.

Zhang jia zupu 張家族譜. With a preface by eleventh-generation descendent Zhang Shaoqu 紹渠. 1823. Jurong county archive #101–2–61.

Zhang Quan 張銓. *Guoshi jiwen* 國史紀聞. 1620.

Zhang Tingyu 張廷玉 et al., eds. *Mingshi* 明史 (Official history of the Ming dynasty). 1736. Reprint, Beijing: Zhonghua shuju, 1974.

Zhong Xing 鍾惺 (1574–1624). *Ming ji nian bian* 明記編年. 1660 edition in 12 *juan*.

Zhou Mi 周密 (1232–1298). *Qidong yeyu* 齊東野語.

Zhou Bingxiu 周秉繡 (Yuan period) and Zhou Xianjing 周憲敬 (Qing period). *Cishan zhi* 祠山志. Expanded edition 1886. Reprint, Yangzhou: Guangling shushe, 2004.

Zhu Guozhen. *Huang Ming shi gai* 皇明史概. 1632.

Zhu Guozhen 朱國楨. *Yongchuang xiaopin* 湧幢小品. 1621. Reprint, Shanghai: Zhonghua shuju, 1959.

"Zhu shi shi de beiji" 朱氏世德碑記 (Stele on the virtue of the Zhu clan in successive generations). In 1676 *Jurong xianzhi* 1/22 (120); 1750/1900 *Jurong xianzhi* 10/19–20 (742 in 1991 reprint). Translated in part in Chan, "Xie Jin as Propagandist," 89–90.

Zhu Wuyi 朱五义. *Wang Yangming zai Qian shiwen zhuyi* 王阳明在黔诗文注译. Guiyang: Guizhou jiaoyu chubanshe, 1996.

Zhu Yuanzhang. "Jia gua zan" 嘉瓜讚 (In praise of auspicious melons). In his *Ming Taizu yuzhi wenji*. Reprint, Taipei: Taiwan xuesheng shuju, 1965. Also reprinted in Qiang Bocheng et al., eds., *Quan Ming Wen*, vol. 1, Shanghai: Shanghai guji chubanshe, 1994.